SCANDALOUS
S T O R I E S
A SORT OF COMMENTARY ON PARABLES

SCANDALOUS
STORIES
A SORT OF COMMENTARY ON PARABLES

DANIEL EMERY PRICE
& ERICK SORENSEN

1517 Publishing

Published by:
1517 Publishing
PO Box 54032
Irvine, CA 92619-4032

Publisher's Cataloging-In-Publication Data
(Prepared by The Donohue Group, Inc.)

Names: Price, Daniel Emery. | Sorensen, Erick. | Bird, Chad, writer of supplementary textual content.
Title: Scandalous stories : a sort of commentary on parables / by Daniel Emery Price and Erick Sorensen ; [foreword by Chad Bird].
Description: Irvine, CA : 1517 Publishing, an imprint of 1517 the Legacy Project, [2018] | Includes bibliographical references.
Identifiers: ISBN 9781945500824 (softcover) | ISBN 9781945500831 (ebook)
Subjects: LCSH: Jesus Christ—Parables—Commentaries. | Scandals—Religious aspects—Christianity.
Classification: LCC BT375.3 .P75 2018 (print) | LCC BT375.3 (ebook) | DDC 226.806—dc23

Cover design by Brenton Clarke Little

1517 Publishing is a boutique publishing house focused on producing high-quality, theological resources to fuel a new Reformation. We promote the defense of the Christian faith, the distinction between law and gospel, vocation and civil courage, and the proclamation of Christ crucified for you.

Printed in the United States of America

that Christ is the interpretation of scripture. The Word made flesh is also the Word forged into our key.

"Aha!" or "Wait, what?"

We might suppose that if any of the rooms in the house of Scripture were already unlocked, with the doors swinging wide open, it would be the parables of Jesus. After all, when teachers employ stories that compare A to B, or illustrate the abstract by means of the concrete, they're attempting to clarify and not cloud the meaning. By using illustrations, teachers are trying to give their students an "Aha!" moment, not elicit a "Wait, what?" response. The story itself is meant to open the door to a confusing or challenging subject.

But as Robert F. Capon reminds us, that's not how rabbi Jesus rolls. With him, "the device of parabolic utterance is used not to explain things to people's satisfaction but to call attention to the unsatisfactoriness of all their previous explanations and understandings."[1] His parables are designed to "pop every circuit breaker in their minds."[2] And he pops those circuit breakers one by one, parable after parable, by telling the kind of stories indicated in the title of this book: scandalous ones.

We often hear parables defined as "earthly stories with a heavenly meaning." But that's not only too simplistic; it's misleading. To begin with, the parables are not your predictable earthly story where good guys finish first, bad guys finish last, and the dashing hero rides off into the sunset with the beauty queen smiling beside him. Very often in the parables of Jesus, the good guy doesn't get the girl; he gets the shaft. The man with a black hat receives a standing ovation, and the unwashed riffraff of society is scooped up from the gutter and plopped down at the head of a king's table with a T-bone steak and a glass of Merlot. These may be earthly stories, but they read more like immorality tales.

Second, the parables aren't about a heavenly, other-worldly meaning. Their subject is the kingdom of God, to be sure, but a kingdom packed with dirt and trees and water and bread and wine and truckloads of twisted sinners. The divine kingdom is a dirty kingdom, rooted in the stuff of creation. The parables don't point "up there," to celestial tru-isms worthy of angelic musings, but "down here," to the crea-tion infused with the promises of the Lamb slain from the foundation of the world. Rather than "earthly stories with a heavenly meaning," the parables are bass-ackward tales with a cruciform meaning. Luther once said that everything that belong to God must be crucified. That applies to the para-bles, too. They are crucified stories.

Crucified Stories

Paul wrote to the Corinthians, "For Jews demand signs and Greeks seek wisdom, but we preach Christ crucified, a stumbling block [Greek: *skandalon*] to Jews and folly to Gentiles, but to those who are called, both Jews and Greeks, Christ the power of God and the wisdom of God" (1 Cor. 1:22–24). Christ crucified is a "stumbling block," a *skand-alon*. The cross of Jesus is indeed scandalous. It is a stum-bling block that trips people up, elicits a disgust response, leaves a bad taste in our spiritual mouths. I mean, what kind of God would sink so low as to die the filthy death of the bad guy, to be smeared with public shame, to present himself to the world as the greatest loser, to breathe his last breath in between two lowlifes? What kind of God would do such a scandalous thing?

The same kind of God who walked around telling scandalous stories, that's who. Stories, for instance, in which a highly respected theological leader, famous for his piety, a churchman who mommas want their babies to grow up and emulate, is held up by Jesus as nothing but a religious blowhard who is so full of himself there's no room for God in him (Luke 18:9–14). And in this same story, Jesus drags onto the stage a sleazy crook, who's stabbed his own countrymen in the back, from whom no decent religious person would accept a friend request, who only mumbles, "God, be merciful to me, the sinner!"—this poor excuse for a human being is the very one that Jesus says his Father will exalt. Now that goes against the grain of everything we want to believe about a score-keeping, good-works-counting, sin-tallying God. It's not only scandalous but insulting to our deepest religious sensibilities. In other words, it's one more example of Jesus crucifying his own stories, telling parables that are a stumbling block to Jews, foolishness to Gentiles, and infuriating to all of us who imagine ourselves on heaven's list of good boys and girls.

And that story is only the proverbial tip of the iceberg. The parables upend all our notions of a God who plays by our rules, who throws parties for valedictorians and shuns the flunkies, who applauds all the good people and laughs at losers. The parables deconstruct those stories by telling scandalous ones. The scandal of the father who welcomes home the prodigal son without exacting a pound of flesh from him, putting him on probation, or even letting him finish his well-rehearsed speech of repentance and self-restoration. He treats this shameful, dirty, pig-smelling embarrassment like he's a king! Throws the biggest shin-dig the community has ever seen in his honor. Now that's not the way things are supposed to work in this world. That's not how good, respectable gods act. Very true, Jesus says. But I'm not a respectable Messiah. I'm a scandalous Messiah, who's come to wreck every fictional notion you treasure about the divine kingdom. In my Father's kingdom, he says, the last are first, the first are last, and only the dead are ready to be made alive.

The Story Beneath All Stories

The eleven parables that Daniel and Erick discuss are a helpful sampling of the wide range of stories that Jesus told about the kingdom of God. Everything from seeds sown all over the place, to outrageous debts forgiven, to a religious heretic serving as first responder to a half-dead mugging victim. What you will not find, however, is any inkling that these stories are about you.

Here's a good rule of thumb: if you find yourself as the hero of any parable, you're doing it wrong. The kingdom in these parables is a kingdom of grace—that is to say, a kingdom of crucifixion, of scandal, of upside-down theology. The only hero of the parables is the messianic madman who gives away the gold of forgiveness like it's candy; who hides oceans of grace in a drop of faith; and who continually crowns the last, the least, the little, and the lifeless. The king in this kingdom is a servant, who comes to give his life as a ransom for many. Indeed, he comes to reveal that, in God's eyes, the ransom was paid long, long ago. From the foundation of the world, he was the sacrifice, the victim, the Lamb. He is the seed of life sown all the world, who bears within himself all the life and fruitfulness of the Father. He is the mystery, hidden from ages ago, who manifests himself in the flesh as the Son of Man who comes to tell scandalous stories, die a scandalous death, and be raised again to fill all with his scandalous grace.

Matthew, quoting from the psalms, says that Jesus opened his mouth in parables that he might utter "what has been hidden since the foundation of the world" (13:35; Ps. 78:2). This hidden story has always the story hiding beneath the surface of all the other biblical stories: creation, the fall, the wanderings of Abraham, the exodus of Israel, all the way through the judges and kings and prophets. There are many stories but really just one story: the parable of the

God who won't turn his back on humanity. Who keeps on pursuing his lost sheep, throwing parties for runaways, eating and drinking with social and religious pariahs. It's the old, old story of the friend of sinners who would rather lose heaven and earth than one of his children. That's *the Story* of which the parables form one part. The story hidden from the foundation of the world, but publicly displayed atop a cross in the grand and gory epiphany where God pulled open his chest to reveal a heart that beats with an undying love for us.

And that scandalous story is worth telling, and retelling, for there's no better—or more important—story in the world.

Notes

1   Robert F. Capon, *Kingdom, Grace, Judgment: Paradox, Outrage, and Vindication in the Parables of Jesus* (Grand Rapids, MI: Eerdmans, 2002), 5.

2   Ibid., 7.

Every Pharisee
Needs a Prostitute

One of the Pharisees asked him [Jesus] to eat with him, and he went into the Pharisee's house and reclined at the table. And behold, a woman of the city, who was a sinner, when she learned that he was reclining at table in the Pharisee's house, brought an alabaster flask of ointment, and standing behind him at his feet, weeping, she began to wet his feet with her tears and wiped them with the hair of her head and kissed his feet and anointed them with the ointment. Now when the Pharisee who had invited him saw this, he said to himself, "If this man were a prophet, he would have known who and what sort of woman this is who is touching him, for she is a sinner." And Jesus answering said to him, "Simon, I have something to say to you." And he answered, "Say it, Teacher." "A certain moneylender had two debtors. One owed five hundred denarii, and the other fifty. When they could not pay, he cancelled the debt of both. Now which of them will love him more?" Simon answered, "The one, I suppose, for whom he cancelled the larger debt." And he said to him, "You have judged rightly." Then turning toward the woman he said to Simon, "Do you see this woman? I entered your house; you gave me no water for my feet, but she has wet my feet with her tears and wiped them with her hair. You gave me no kiss, but from the time I came in she has not ceased to kiss my feet. You did not anoint my head with oil, but she has anointed my feet with ointment. Therefore, I tell you, her sins, which are many, are forgiven—for she loved much. But he who is forgiven little, loves little." And he said to her, "Your sins are forgiven." Then those who were at table with him began to say among themselves, "Who is this, who even forgives sins?" And he said to the woman, "Your faith has saved you; go in peace."

—Luke 7:36–50

It's not just the words Jesus says that are overly scandalous but often the places where he says them and the people he says them to. This is one such occasion.

"Jesus ate with sinners." We hear this all the time, and it's true. Jesus hung out with some unsavory people. Partied with some lowlifes. Dined with many a degenerate. Depending on your view of yourself, this may be offensive or comforting. I tend to vacillate between the two depending on how righteous I'm feeling moment to moment on any particular day. Such is the pendulum-swinging life of the sinner/saint.

But Jesus also ate with Pharisees. Pharisees are sinners too. Seems like Jesus was willing to be seen with anyone. He accepted invitations from the religious elite and the socially outcast alike—those in the church and those outside of it. But whether he was fine dining with chief priests or multiplying fish and bread with tax collectors, he was likely telling stories while he did it.

In the seventh chapter of Luke's gospel, we see these two worlds collide with Jesus at the center. Jesus has been invited to Simon the Pharisee's house for a meal, and as usual he accepts. He arrives. They eat. And as they are hanging out after dinner (reclining at the table), a woman enters the house. Now, this isn't one of the guests' wives or daughters. This isn't a servant or a hired maid. This is "a women of the city, a sinner." That's some title. There is a difference between being a woman *from* the city and being a woman *of* the city.

There is nothing strange or offensive about living in the city, but this woman earned her living in the shadows. She sold herself to others under the cover of darkness, not to hide her shame (which seemed to be well known) but to hide the shame of her clients. She was an outlet for all the lusts of the human heart to be poured into. She would bear the shame of your sin for a price. Her clients walked freely in the daylight. They were invited to social gatherings and dinner parties. They were welcome in the house of worship. And no one knew.

What happened with her was known by all, but with whom it happened stayed with her. Her lips were sealed. All this earned her the undesirable label "woman *of* the city." Initially no one said anything. Perhaps it was out of shock that this woman would dare enter this house. This was the house of a man of God. What if someone saw her enter? What would they think? Rumors and gossip would no doubt snowball out of control. It seemed Simon was waiting to see if Jesus would object to this outrageous disruption. Was he on team righteous or team unrighteous? Surely "a prophet" would dismiss her. Rebuke her. Chastise her.

Then things go from outrageous audacity to scandalous defilement as she drops to her knees weeping. Her tears cover the feet of Jesus, and she begins to dry them with her hair. And the unthinkable happens. She begins to kiss his feet as she applies expensive ointment to them. Jesus was allowing lips that committed countless sins to touch his skin with affection. Lips that could testify against countless unfaithful and promiscuous men met his dirty feet. As she was anointing them with ointment purchased with money earned in fornication and adultery.

Whatever good thoughts Simon had of Jesus just vanished. *This man is no prophet of God. A prophet would know who this woman is*—what *this woman is! No righteous man would allow this!* These are the thoughts of a horrified Pharisee, and Jesus knew them all.

We love it when Jesus lays a public smack down on the private thoughts of a Pharisee (as long as it's not the Pharisee in the mirror). But that isn't the main thing happening here. Simon is questioning everything about Jesus. He doesn't believe him to be the Son of God or even a prophet of God. This event has him believing Jesus was quite the opposite. This Jesus was an imposter. A false prophet. An antinomian[1] who cared nothing about God's law or sin. These were blasphemous thoughts and opinions to have about the Son of God and deserved a stern rebuke. Instead Jesus sought to make the offended Pharisee understand a fundamental truth about the God he had devoted his life to studying, worshiping, and serving.

Jesus did this in a four-sentence story—a thirty-three-word parable about two people who owed a debt to the same person. One owed significantly more than the other, but neither could pay. So this generous man forgave them both. The story is that simple and ends with a question: "Which one will love him more?"

This is no riddle. The answer to the question is obvious—so obvious even the most wrongheaded Pharisee can get it right and does. You could have answered correctly, and so could I. The question behind the question is: "Which one are you Simon?" Which one are we? Not which one do we think we are. Not which one do we act like. The question is: are we people who owe a great debt or a small one?

Jesus says those who have been forgiven much, love much, and those who have been forgiven little, love little. The truth is, no one needs to be forgiven only a little. There are no small debtors. There are those who are great debtors and know it and those who are great debtors and think or pretend they are small ones. The Law of God bends for no one. This same Jesus who is having his feet washed in tears of shame and kissed with lips of secrets is the same Jesus who said:

> "You have heard that it was said, 'You shall not commit adultery.' But I say to you that everyone who looks at a woman with lustful intent has already committed adultery with her in his heart." (Matthew 5:27–28)

Simon never sought this woman out in the city at night. His name was not among the secrets she kept. He never paid her to have the sins of his heart moved to his hands. But Jesus wasn't only reading Simon's thoughts; he was exegeting his heart. And his heart betrayed his perceived righteousness (and our hearts do the same).

Outwardly we white knuckle abstinence from any number of besetting sins, but we have not and cannot change the intentions of our hearts. We believe resisting evil has earned us something or at least it better qualifies us for holy things. We think we can invite Jesus over just as we are. We think we're righteous enough. We need not weep, wail, or worship. We don't believe we have sins that demand a response like that.

The Pharisee will always stand tall in the presence of Jesus. With chest out, chin up, and heart hidden, we invite God over for dinner as our equal. It's no wonder we are all horrified when all our hidden thoughts come walking through our door uninvited.

The Offence of Our Heart on Another's Sleeve

We don't love little because we have little that requires forgiveness. We love little because we've confessed little and hidden much. Therefore we experience little forgiveness. This is what Jesus is teaching both Simon and us when he says, "I tell you, her sins, which are many, are forgiven—for she loved much" (v. 47).

This is not to say that her great love resulted in her forgiveness, but rather such great love is evidence she has been forgiven much. This is further shown in the following statement: "But he who is forgiven little, loves little." (v. 47).

No amount of Law keeping or straight and narrow walking can produce love in us. Forgiveness alone does that. Free grace alone serves as water for the parched, cracked soil of the human heart. When this kind of water is poured out the Holy Spirit brings forth the fruit of the Spirit.[2]

Simon doesn't need to go out and find a prostitute, sleep with her, and then return to Jesus for forgiveness to have this love produced in him. He needs to be confronted with the reality that his own heart is every bit a "thing *of* the city" as this woman. No one can out-sin the fallen human heart.

We wrongly assume the desires we suppress magically turn into holiness—a sort of meritorious abstinence. We try not sin so we can be good enough to invite God over for dinner. We need to stop. This will never work. The Maker and Knower of hearts isn't buying it. He'll accept our invitation to come over for dinner. He's too good and gracious not to. And if we're lucky, a woman of the street will crash our party. When the things we desperately try to hide are weeping in our dining room it's a jarring, self-righteous horror. But it's definitely something we need. Jesus loves this woman of countless sins enough to forgive her, and he loves this Pharisee of nameless sins enough to absolve her in front of him.

The offense of seeing someone forgiven of everything we're striving and striving to suppress, right in front of us, cannot be overlooked. We wouldn't dare lay our lips on this man. It's unthinkable. Maybe that's because we don't know him well enough. We're too busy trying to impress him with the shine of our fine china, the true north of our moral compass, and the true right angle of our uncorrupted theology to get to know the heart of this friend of sinners from Nazareth.

The uncomfortable truth is that Jesus doesn't come to be wined and dined by the righteous. He comes to forgive debts (there are no small debts) and invite us to the blessed after party that never ends. But first he comes to make us uncomfortable in the best way. He comes to make us desperately dependent on the only thing that ultimately delivers from death—himself.

The Tyranny of Little Love vs. Jesus

Jesus is radically different. He is not a king who demands you come before him trembling and begging, making you kiss his ring and feet to acquire mercy for the debts you owe. That kind of king is in need of your submission to validate his authority. You are just a pawn in his power play of human strength.

"Little-love" is a tyrant. He rules the kingdom of our hearts he inherited from his father, "Little-to-be-forgiven." He is merciless and cold. He is never wrong and views compassion as weakness. He's the kind of tyrant who breaks every mirror in his kingdom so he never has to look at his true reflection. He replaces them all with paintings of himself in his finest hours. Little-love cannot give. He doesn't have enough. He never has enough. He can only take.

This is not Jesus. Jesus comes to give. Jesus comes to serve. He comes to forgive unspeakable sins—sins that shock us when they invade the safe place of our clean lives. He comes to become them. To assume them into himself. He doesn't forgive out of an empty bank account. With every act of forgiveness, a transaction is made. Our is sin exchanged for his righteousness. This sin will be paid for, bled for, died for, and left in a barrowed tomb.

> Greater love has no one than this, that someone lay down his life for his friends. (John 15:13)

The big love of Jesus can give forever and never run dry. But because we live from a position of lack, we cannot fathom that anyone has enough love, grace, and goodness to fill up the account of even just one *real* sinner (never mind a whole world of them). So we actively try to show we're not overly deficient. We push to the front of the line, walk right up, and present ourselves as one who needs only the smallest amount of grace. Our list of sins is short, and none of them are the really bad ones. As if to say: "Just top us off, Jesus. We've done pretty well." We have little that requires forgiveness. This is how we got here. This is how Simon got there. And this is how we all become ruled by Little-love.

Witnesses of Absolution

We are happy with a Jesus who forgives tame sins of the almost-righteous. It's the forgiveness of such wild sins *of* the city that scandalize us. The sins "out there." The sins of the culture going to hell in a hand basket. The sins we think we haven't committed. The transgression of the laws we falsely convince ourselves we're keeping. The love of God comes as an unwelcome assault on all our attempts to show him a good time.

This is an unwelcome and undeserved grace to us. The forgiveness of everything we hide, right in front of our eyes. She doesn't say a word. There are no excuses. No flowery words of "true repentance" are spoken for the Pharisee to evaluate. Not a single word is spoken by this woman, and the only word spoken to her is one of absolution. She names no names. She casts no blame. Her lips utter no accusation against the ones who availed themselves of her services. She exposes no sin of her accomplices.

Absolution has done its finished work, and her lips are busy with the freed work of affection toward her forgiver. Tragically the guests at this dinner are indignant. The complete absolution of *that* sin (insert whatever sin it may be for you) is too scandalous. Who does this man think he is? To forgive sins at all is blasphemous. To forgive *those* sins is unthinkable. And to forgive them without a word is downright offensive. We need to be offended by Jesus—to stumble over a word of grace to the worst of our fellow sinners.

The little love of the Pharisee always rejects the free forgiveness and acceptance of the sinner. This free gift is a battering ram against the doors of our hallowed dining halls of faux righteousness. Yet Jesus enters this merciful siege of our self-made kingdom—not to take captives but to set them free saying, "Your sins are forgiven. Go in peace."

May God be so gracious to send a woman *of* the city to every party we throw for Jesus.

Notes

1   Antinomian: of or relating to the view that Christians are released by grace from the obligation of observing the moral law.
2   See Titus 3:4–7 and Gal. 5:22–23.

An Unimpressive Kingdom

He said therefore, "What is the kingdom of God like? And to what shall I compare it? It is like a grain of mustard seed that a man took and sowed in his garden, and it grew and became a tree, and the birds of the air made nests in its branches." And again he said, "To what shall I compare the kingdom of God? It is like leaven that a woman took and hid in three measures of flour, until it was all leavened."

—Luke 13:18–21

The story's told that to intimidate his enemy, Darius, king of Persia, sent Alexander the Great a bag of sesame seeds, meant to suggest the imposing number of Darius's troops and the power of his kingdom. Not to be outdone in the intimidation game, Alexander then sent Darius a bag of mustard seeds to display his kingdom's strength. Why? Because not only were mustard seeds more numerous due to their smaller size, but they were also more potent and fiery.

I suppose when we read the parable before us about God's kingdom being like a mustard seed thrown into a garden, our most natural desire would be to think of it in this way. His kingdom is like a vast army of powerful soldiers that are so numerous that they are here to take over the world for him. But as much as we might want to believe that's what's being presented about the kingdom, from the context of the rest of the kingdom parables, it's abundantly clear that this is not it. Indeed, as his disciples and everyone around him find out, the kingdom of God does not come in the way we expect. In fact, God's kingdom comes in ways we don't tend to like. That fact has not changed even to this day.

God's Kingdom Operates from the Outside

When Jesus taught his disciples how to pray, one of the first things he told them in the Lord's Prayer was to ask for God's kingdom to come and for his will to be done. What's implicit in this command is that God's kingdom is not naturally inside any of us. Oh I know, it's popular in new-agey type circles to talk about us having a "spark of the divine" (and it is true that human beings are created in his image), but the biblical perspective is that little light of ours has been snuffed out. In it of ourselves we're in the dark (John 3:19, 2 Cor. 4:4). In fact, what Jesus says comes from within is just the opposite of divine: "evil thoughts, sexual immorality, theft murder, adultery, coveting, wickedness, deceit, sensuality, envy, slander, pride, and foolishness" (Mark 7:21–22). No human being naturally has God reigning in his or her heart as King. Unfortunately, we bear the marks of our first parents, Adam and Eve, who, through their disobedience to God, essentially chose to try to usurp the throne of God rather than submit to him as their Sovereign.

Every time we do something that we know God has said not to do, or dwell on thoughts God has said not to think, or say the things we ought not say, we show that naturally we do not possess the kingdom within. Especially in the highly individualistic West, the idea of a king telling us how to live seems like an affront to our very definition of self. So the scripture says naturally, "There is no one who seeks God, no, not one." Like a child who refuses to eat their veggies, so too we do not submit to God's rule in our lives. So, like the garden, like the bread, the mustard seed and the yeast of his kingdom must be planted in us by his Spirit from the outside.

The good news for us is that to save his creation, God does graciously plant the seed of his word and mixes in the yeast of his kingdom in our lives. It is entirely external. Our righteousness is no righteousness at all. As the prophet Isaiah says, even our good deeds are as filthy rags in God's sight, because they are still stained with sin (Isa. 64:6). We need a separate righteousness, a perfect righteousness that none of us has.

None of us, that is, except for Jesus. By his amazing grace through faith, God exchanges our unrighteousness for the righteousness of Jesus Christ. He plants it in the garden and places it in the bread of our souls. This is why Paul exclaims with excitement in Romans 3:21–22, "But now the righteousness of God has been manifested *apart from our natural works*, the righteousness of God through faith in Jesus Christ for all who believe."

So you say, "Awesome! Through faith in Jesus, I have the Creator's almighty presence within me. Nothing can stop me now." Well . . . Not so fast . . . Because even though we possess God's Spirit (or better, God's Spirit possesses us), our parables show us that God's kingdom doesn't look all that impressive (at least at first).

An Unimpressive Kingdom

Have you ever seen a mustard seed? If you have, you know it's pretty tiny. When deciding how to describe the kingdom to us, Jesus purposely used the smallest known seed at the time. The leaven is hardly anything in comparison to the amount of dough it is placed into.

Surely this picture of the kingdom of God must have been disappointing to the disciples gathering around Jesus. No doubt most of them were staking their lives on the idea that Jesus was the Jewish Messiah, and as Jewish Messiah, he was going to raise up a large army, kick out the imperialist Roman powers, and set up his throne to rule a world of peace forever (with them in positions of power next to him, of course). The kingdom is like a mighty redwood tree—that's better! Strong, impossible to cut down, and imposing. But that is not the picture he uses. Instead, he uses the very unimpressive mustard seed to describe his kingdom, and his disciples have a hard time accepting it.

Over and over throughout the gospel accounts you hear this viewpoint expressed by the disciples. James and John jockey to "sit at his right and left" when he comes in his glory (Mark 10:37). Peter rebukes Jesus when he tells them that he's not going to wear a crown of gold, but a crown of thorns, promising that he'll lay down his life for him before that happens. In every case, Jesus insists that his kingdom isn't going to operate that way. First there will be a cross before a crown.

This description of the apparent smallness of God's kingdom can be disappointing to us as well. When we pray for greatness, and instead he humbles us we're disappointed by his kingdom. We would like God to rule by placing just the right leaders in political office so they can pass laws to make our country "great again," but it doesn't happen. The constant temptation is to try to bring the kingdom from the top down rather than the bottom up. But that's not how God's kingdom operates.

Helmut Thielicke was a pastor in Germany during the height of World War II. He illustrates the smallness of the kingdom of God for us well:

When I became a Pastor and conducted my first Bible-Study hour I went into it with the determination to trust in Jesus saying: "All power is given unto me in heaven and in earth." I said these words to myself in order to assure myself that even Hitler, who was then in the saddle, and his dreadful power machine were merely puppets hanging by strings in the hands of this mighty Lord. And in the Bible study hour I was faced by two very old ladies and a still older organist. He was a very worthy man, but his fingers were palsied and this was embarrassingly apparent in his playing. So this was the extent of the accomplishment of this Lord, to whom all power in heaven and earth had been given, *supposedly* given. And outside marched the battalions of youth who were subject to altogether different lords. This was all he had to set before me on that evening. What *did* he have to offer anyway? And if it really were nothing more than this—then isn't he refuted by this utterly miserable response?[1]

Well, no, that's just how his kingdom operates. When I was a boy growing up, I never wanted to go to church, except for a short time when I was five or six. The reason I wanted to go at that time is because in the children's ministry there was a young adult named Steve who for some reason took me under his wing. I don't remember anything he said to me, nor do I remember really much about him. All I know is that he had a reddish afro and he was nice to me. And because he was so nice to me, for a short time I actually wanted to come to church. You see, the kingdom of God operates in small, unimpressive ways. I've been reminded of this whenever I listen to my son Lincoln (who is now six years old) praying at night words that don't really go together all that well:

Thank you, God. Thank you, Jesus, for Mommy and Daddy, for my Batman toy, and I want a Batman game. I want a Spiderman toy too. Thank you for dying on the cross. Thank you for my brothers too. Thank you for Chestnut. [That's our dog.] Amen.

The kingdom of God operates in small, seemingly insignificant ways. This is the way it's always been and it always will be until heaven is our permanent home. The first disciples were a ragtag bunch of fishermen, ex tax collectors, and zealots. There were former prostitutes hanging out alongside disgraced pharisees. The people Jesus healed were not people of great cultural influence most of the time, but they were oddballs, strangers, and outcasts. And even our Lord himself had nothing attractive by his nature that would draw us to him (Isaiah 53:2). After all, if we look at it from the perspective of the average person in the first century, there could be nothing seemingly more insignificant than a Jewish man from a small corner of Palestine that was murdered by crucifixion. But that's how the kingdom of God operates. And yet, as unimpressive as it may look, God's kingdom is growing.

A Growing Kingdom

As Jesus goes on to tell us in the parable, the mustard seed starts off tiny and infinitesimal, but grows into the biggest tree in the garden, with birds perching on its branches. The yeast eventually takes over the bread it was placed into. This is also how the kingdom of God operates. Jesus did not simply end up a murdered Jewish rabbi, but he rose from the dead, defeating the powers of the world, the devil, and the flesh. The church was a small, insignificant group of people, but just fifty days after the resurrection of Jesus, it had grown to thousands. By the end of the first century, the mighty Roman empire, who the people so wanted Jesus to defeat, began to decline not by the armies and kings of this world, but by the simple preaching of the good news that Jesus had lived, died, and rose from the dead for the salvation of their souls. Through that message, the Roman empire's hearts were converted and transformed.

Over the last few years, I have worked to plant Epiphany Church in New York City. I can honestly say it has been the most challenging thing I've ever done. *By far.* Attendance is entirely unpredictable and funding is always stressful. Because our church is mainly composed of people in their twenties, it is super transient, so you never know who's moving out when. There have been many days where I've wondered if we're going to make it (however one defines "making it" in this context).

But then I think of Joe. Joe just happened to walk by one day before our worship service as our musicians were practicing. Curious, Joe came in and asked if he could talk to a pastor. He was very nervous and very shy. His voice shaking, he explained to me that he suffered from severe, debilitating anxiety and that to even go outside for him was a struggle. And yet, he had questions about "spiritual things." That first time, he wouldn't stay for the worship service (too many people!), but thankfully, he showed up the following week for Sunday school. Then he did it again. And again. Eventually, after a few months, he pulled me aside and said he believed in Jesus and he wanted to be baptized. I was beside myself with excitement. Joe would be our church's first baptism! And so, a few weeks later, Joe mustered up every bit of courage he had as he stood up in front of the entire church and was baptized in the name of the Father, the Son and the Holy Spirit. God's kingdom is growing. As we preach God's message, he plants his seed in people's hearts. As we gather around his table, he delivers the leaven of his kingdom, and it takes over our lives.

Here's the deal: Oftentimes, you may not sense or feel that God is working his kingdom personally in your life. You still seem to struggle with the same old sins; your attitude doesn't seem to be all that different, but let this parable assure you that he is working. His kingdom may not look as impressive as you would expect, but he's not done. Trust him, because his word declares this awesome truth: "He who began a good work in you will bring it to completion at the day of Jesus Christ."

Note

1 Thielicke, Helmut, & John W. Doberstein. The Waiting Father, Lutterworth Press, Cambridge, 1957, pp 62

Putting Down the Scythe

He put another parable before them, saying, "The kingdom of heaven may be compared to a man who sowed good seed in his field, but while his men were sleeping, his enemy came and sowed weeds among the wheat and went away. So when the plants came up and bore grain, then the weeds appeared also. And the servants of the master of the house came and said to him, 'Master, did you not sow good seed in your field? How then does it have weeds?' He said to them, 'An enemy has done this.' So the servants said to him, 'Then do you want us to go and gather them?' But he said, 'No, lest in gathering the weeds you root up the wheat along with them. Let both grow together until the harvest, and at harvest time I will tell the reapers, Gather the weeds first and bind them in bundles to be burned, but gather the wheat into my barn.'"

—Matthew 13:24–30

Tony wasn't the answer I wanted when I was asking God to grow our church. We needed some more stable families. We were a young church filled with young people. As the pastor I was asking God to send us some older people. People with more grey hair. Some people with steady jobs. A few saints who had their act together. People who could contribute. Some seasoned veterans in the faith.

Tony wasn't any of those things. He was in-between jobs. He exceled at making everyone feel uncomfortable. He kept making terrible decision after terrible decision, in every aspect of life. Yet he showed up to church every Sunday slurping on a seventy-two-ounce cup/cooler of soda all service long, while never taking his hat off (which shouldn't have bothered as much as it did). Tony got a job. Tony lost a job. Tony got married. Tony got divorced. After many conversations that went nowhere, I remember thinking, *This guy just doesn't get it. Why does he keep coming here?* God gives us strange gifts.

The Bible is full of stories about unlikely saints. They're literally in every book. People who didn't look the part. Didn't act the part. Made mistakes and then made them again. I'm reminded of Abraham's nephew Lot. That guy was a hot mess, living on Main Street in the most wicked city in the world. It was a city so wicked God torched it. When mercy showed up in the form of angels to tell him it was time to get out because destruction is coming . . . he delayed. He didn't want to leave. When he finally did leave, the first thing he did was get drunk and impregnate both his daughters. Can you imagine this guy in your church? What a nightmare! Would you think this man could possibly be a believer? How about "righteous" as an adjective to describe him? That's probably not the first word that comes to mind. Yet that is exactly what the apostle Peter says about him in 2 Peter 2:7–8:

> And if he rescued righteous Lot, greatly distressed by the sensual conduct of the wicked (for as that righteous man lived among them day after day, he was tormenting his righteous soul over their lawless deeds that he saw and heard).

We all know how hard it is not to judge people by what we see with the naked eye. The Prophet Samuel was instructed by God not to judge young David by his appearance. God knows this is what we will always do. So Samuel ignores David's stature. However, if Samuel could have looked into the future, he would have seen much more condemning David than simply being much shorter than the ideal king.

Did David have big victories? Yes. But he also had adultery, murder, disobedience, and family uprisings on his resume. Just as shocking as Lot being called "righteous" is David being called "a man after God's own heart who will do all His will" (Acts 13:22). Really? "*All* his will?" Are we talking about the same David?

It seems every piece of saintly wheat in the scriptures had times where they looked like nothing more than weeds. Sometimes for the majority of their biblical narrative. We should no doubt do away with our notations of "righteousness" or Christian piety when we examine the outward evidence seen all over the lives of Lot, David, Samson, Abraham, Noah, and so on. If these men were in our churches, we surely would have gathered them up as weeds that were ruining the reputation of God and the church and slapped the label "false convert" on each one of them.

The Obsession with the False Convert

> God's people and the Church are those who rely on nothing else than God's grace and mercy.
> —Martin Luther[1]

If I had a dollar for every time someone asked me, "Do you think _____ is saved?" Or said, "I'm not even sure _____ is a believer," I could buy a small island and retire. Few things get my eyes rolling faster than talking about false converts—not because such a thing doesn't exist but because we have an unhealthy obsession with it. We are like the servants of the master in the parable. We run around trying to identify weeds in the field of the church to gather them up and toss them out. We weigh their every word and action. We dissect their motives and intentions. We hear the church is to be without "spot or wrinkle" (Eph. 5:27), and in misplaced zeal, we take this task upon ourselves. We identify spots to remove and wrinkles to run over with the hot iron of reproof. We do all these things thinking we're doing God and his church a great service. And Jesus knows we are prone to this. This is why he gives us this parable.

God Wasn't Taking a Nap

We must not think the point of this story is the devil has secretly planted people in our churches. There isn't a worse construction you could put on someone than "the seed of Satan." If that is the point we walk away with, it will make us skeptical of all our neighbors. We will judge them ruthlessly. We will look for reasons to reject them as brothers and sisters. We need no aid in this work. We do this by default. We are naturally and sinfully bent toward putting the worst construction on everything and everyone. A focus on the devil will always result in weed identifying and gathering. Jesus is not trying to bolster any of that.

Being devil centered will also get us busy with the work of trying to look like wheat. If we're on the lookout for weeds, we think others are too. We'll feel an overwhelming pressure to prove to them that we should not be gathered up and tossed out. We will try to walk like wheat and talk like wheat. We will become obsessed with our goodness and everyone else's badness. Our rightness and their wrongness. And we're sure to confuse our rightness with righteousness every time.

When we hear there are weeds among the wheat, we have a terrible habit of looking for the sinners. The problem is, everywhere we look, all we see is sinners. It turns out sinners are all that there are. Sinners on the left and wretches on the right.

Some people have heard the good news that Christ was born to take the sins of the world upon himself. That he lived a perfect life in our place and then went to the cross to die in our place. Then after being dead for three days, he rose again. They have heard that they are freely justified before God because of Christ and Christ alone. And they believe it. That is what makes a Christian. And all those who confess this are still sinners. The difference between the sinner who believes and the sinner who doesn't is in the believing not in the sinning. This is what Martin Luther called being *Simul Justus et Peccator* (Simultaneously Justified and Sinner). Believe me, I know some outwardly righteous pagans and some really dirty Christians. So this outward examination of weeds and wheat won't provide the distinctions we're looking for.

The shocking truth is, Jesus doesn't say weeds who look like wheat are the primary problem. This isn't why he tells the servants not to gather them up. Jesus doesn't share our fear of having unbelievers sitting in pews next to believers. Read it again. The reason he gives is this: we cannot be trusted not to throw out rough-looking wheat along with the weeds. Jesus knows wheat can look a whole lot like weeds when we are judging it before his final harvest.

Our obsession with keeping the church pure and clean is an outright denial of how very weed-like we all look at times. We've all had days, months, years, or even decades where we are swiftly cut down by zealous "servants" on a mission to purge the field. Countless splits and schisms in the body of Christ find their roots in this self-righteousness and false purity. Every new church tries to figure out a way to be purer than the church before it. A way to have less weeds and more wheat. A church with less substance abuse, porn addiction, adultery, divorce, and every other easily identifiable grossly "unchristian" weed-like behavior. But what we end up with is a congregation of people lying to themselves. An assembly of the self-deceived.

> Farewell to those who want an entirely pure and purified church. This is plainly wanting no church at all.
> —Martin Luther[2]

The Grace of Growing up with Weeds

It's important to note that the weeds were sown in the field while the master's men slept, not the master. This catches them by surprise, but not him. Nothing surprises God. He was not alarmed, nor was he unwilling to have it happen. It happens while the servants are asleep by his design. God doesn't wish for this to be stopped. Both history and experience show we would most certainly try to stop it. While we slumber, God allows the devil to do this, and by doing so, the devil has unwittingly been used by God.

One reason people don't pull up weeds before the harvest is that plants sharing the same soil will have their roots so intertwined that if you uproot one, you may pull up others with it. Could it be that Jesus wants our roots and lives that intimately intertwined? Yes. For now, God wants both wheat and weeds growing up together. He wants us rubbing up against what we'd rather not be close to. He wants us pulling them in, not pushing them out—to be intimately involved in the lives of faithless people, to the point where if they were taken from us, it would pull at the very depths of our souls. It would tug at our roots.

This is a grace not only to them and maybe not even primarily to them. It's a grace to us. It's the ever-present opportunity to exercise the freedom to love and extend mercy to people Christ cares for deeply. What may one day be burned up must in the here and now be seen as objects of mercy.

We cannot clean ourselves up by removing everything dirty from our presence. God doesn't want us that deceived. Here is someone to love; they're not a Christian. They're not very clean and don't seem to care. Love them. Let your life become intertwined with theirs. Let it cost you something. This is a grace that will not let you stray too far from sinners, lest you start to believe you are no longer one.

When Weeds Become Wheat

There are few things in scripture more clear than the condition and family we were all born in.

> And you were dead in the trespasses and sins in which you once walked, following the course of this world, following the prince of the power of the air, the spirit that is now at work in the sons of disobedience—among whom we all once lived in the passions of our flesh, carrying out the desires of the body and the mind, and were by nature children of wrath, like the rest of mankind. (Ephesians 2:1–3)
>
> [Jesus] came to his own, and his own people did not receive him. But to all who did receive him, who believed in his name, he gave the right to become children of God, who were born, not of blood nor of the will of the flesh nor of the will of man, but of God. (John 1:12–13)

Dead in sins, children of wrath, people needing adoption, etc. These are the phrases the scriptures use to describe each and every one of us. The family categories are: children of wrath/the devil (weeds) and children of God (wheat).

And all are born in the former. This means a transfer must take place. A transformation. An adoption.

> [God] has delivered us from the domain of darkness and transferred us to the kingdom of his beloved Son, in whom we have redemption, the forgiveness of sins. (Colossians 1:13–14)

The biblical reality is that sometimes weeds become wheat. In fact, all wheat were formerly weeds. This transformation doesn't happen through weeds trying harder to be like wheat. It doesn't happen by weeds shaping up, acting better, or being more devoted. And it most certainly doesn't happen by cutting them down and casting them out. So we can put away our judgmental evaluation of the person in the pew across from us and our critical assessment of all our neighbors. It seems we are in need of constant reminding that this transformation happens by the grace of God. It happens through the good news that because of the finished work of Christ, all may come and be part of the good master's harvest, just as they are. To become wheat, you must come as a weed.

We were all weeds once. We are weeds who have been adopted by God and transferred from the domain of darkness into the kingdom of Christ (Colossians 1:13–14). You would think this would make us a generous and gracious people—people full of compassion and empathy for those not yet in the family of grace. That we would be overcome with the desire to draw them near and not let them go until they too have been adopted. That we would love them in such a way that it would devastate us to see them leave or be cut down. That the knowledge of who we once were and the kingdom in which we once lived would keep us from turning up our noses or looking with a skeptical eye at those around us. So often it has not. We still want to compare ourselves to everyone else. We're looking for someone to judge—someone dirtier than we perceive ourselves to be. Someone we can feel "holy" next to (but not too close).

It seems we are poor handlers of grace. We are restless. We struggle to believe we are wheat simply because God says so. We are skeptical of our own unconditional adoption, and we wrestle with the lie that we have something to prove to our Father. Our constant evaluation of others is rooted in our own insecurity as one transferred into the kingdom of God's Son. Yet all this grappling with the radical grace of God doesn't diminish it. It's still hunting down both us and the people we're not quite sure are part of us. God is still in the business of turning weeds into wheat.

Are there weeds among us? Jesus says there are. But the wheat is looking pretty rough, and I'm not about to try and separate the two. It's not harvest time, and God isn't cutting down anything yet. Let's put away the scythe. With it we don't look Jesus; we look like the grim reaper.

Coming Full Circle

Tony wasn't what I was praying for. But he *is* what I needed. I pray every church is graced with as many Tonys as it takes to teach them the lesson of this parable. The people we didn't ask for, who appear out of nowhere when we're sleeping, they are gifts to be received, sinners to be loved, and unknowing teachers of the profound truths of God.

So what happened to Tony? Did he finally "get it"? Did he shape up or turn his life around? Is he now a deacon or leading a men's ministry? Or did he lose yet another job? Divorce another wife and get addicted to another drug? Did he leave the church altogether? You don't need to know. Sorry. You'd just use that information to determine whether he is a weed or a wheat. We all would. So who is Tony? Tony is someone put in the field either by God or with God's eyes wide open. A gift. Someone to love. That's enough. Let's leave the scythe in the barn.

Notes

1 Ewald M. Pless, *What Luther Says.* (St. Louis, MO: Concordia Publishing House, 1959), 256.
2 Ibid., 272

Bringing Fruit out of the Dirt

Most of the time, it must have been pretty exhilarating to walk as a disciple of Jesus. You would see him heal blindness one day and the next day watch him provide hearing to a man for the first time. On another day you might witness him bring back a person from the dead or provide meals for thousands with just a couple fish and a few loaves. And then there were those times when you quietly laughed to yourself as he confronted religious bullies or shed a tear as he embraced life's losers.

But then . . . walking with Jesus must have been confusing too. You know he has the power to overthrow Rome, but he keeps on insisting he'll lay down his power to be overthrown on a cross. You believe he's the Son of God, but the ministry's being funded by female benefactors (Luke 8:1–3). And what is up with his parables? Sometimes he just tells a story out of the blue with no context, no introductions, no hints and then stops. Like this one:

> That same day Jesus went out of the house and sat beside the sea. And great crowds gathered about him, so that he got into a boat and sat down. And the whole crowd stood on the beach. And he told them many things in parables, saying: "A sower went out to sow. And as he sowed, some

seeds fell along the path, and the birds came and devoured them. Other seeds fell on rocky ground, where they did not have much soil, and immediately they sprang up, since they had no depth of soil, but when the sun rose they were scorched. And since they had no root, they withered away. Other seeds fell among thorns, and the thorns grew up and choked them. Other seeds fell on good soil and produced grain, some a hundredfold, some sixty, some thirty. He who has ears, let him hear." (Matthew 13:1–9)

Ummm . . . what? That's the parable? Chances are many of us are familiar with this parable, and we've heard its meaning explained, but picture being in that crowd that day. What on earth is he trying to tell us? He just launches into a story about a guy throwing out seed and how certain kinds of soils respond. It's no wonder that in the very next verse, his disciples are like, "Umm, why are you talking in parables? What question are you trying to answer here?" Thankfully, Jesus eventually explains what he's talking about (sometimes he doesn't!). He tells us that the Sower represents God (or one of his representatives) and that the seed represents the word of the kingdom (or in other words, the word about Jesus). The soils represent four different kinds of hearers of this word.

Hard Soil

This guy is pretty cynical about religion. Like the hardened path, he's been walked on before, and he's pretty sure that Christianity is a sham. He's seen the dudes pleading for money on "Christian" television, promising that God will bless him "tenfold" if he just gives a little more toward their super important private jet, and he knows what they're really up to. Sure, he's heard the story of Jesus and how he died for his sins, but he's not even sure that Jesus really existed. Here's the thing: he's not particularly angry about it either. I mean, he's not like one of those shrill "new atheists." He's just indifferent to the whole thing; apathy suits him just fine when it comes to the question of God. So the word bounces right off of him, in one ear and out the other.

It is true that this guy did pray as a kid. He actually grew up going to church fairly regularly and was confirmed in the church. He remembers the preacher railing every Sunday about all the moral problems in the world and in the church. (And of course, what happens in a church where a steady diet of rules preaching is received is that people learn how to fake it really well in front of each other.) To him, the church was filled with actors. Everyone seemed to wear their "Sunday best" to hide their Saturday failures. And so at some point (right around the time he left home for college), the man shrugged and decided the whole Christian thing wasn't for him.

The above description is a pretty easy caricature of the hardened soil, but the fact is, it is possible for people to sit in church their whole lives and be in this same place. I mean, that's where so many of the Pharisees of Jesus's day were at, right? They constantly sat under the word of God being taught and sought to memorize every jot and tittle of it; they constantly sought to live their lives outwardly in conformity with God's law. And yet, Jesus calls them "whitewashed tombs filled with dead men's bones" and "hypocrites." Is it possible that you are the hardened soil?

The Rocky Soil

I've met and been friends with numerous people that I'm pretty sure were in this category of hearer. I can remember one friend—we'll call him Lance—who came up to me out of the blue excitedly proclaiming that he had become a Christian. By all outward appearances this man was super enthusiastic. He was waking up every day and spending mass amounts of time reading his Bible; anytime he could pray, he was at it. When we'd go out, it didn't matter who we were with. He was always talking about Jesus with people (God help the person that didn't know Jesus as his Savior yet), often asking if they wanted right then to commit their lives to Jesus because "the days were short." But then . . . something changed. He stopped showing up at church for a few weeks. That was surely understandable. I mean, everyone misses worship sometimes. So I called Lance to see how he was doing, and that fire, that zeal in his voice that had been pervasive just a few weeks earlier was gone. I asked what was going on in his life, and after digging around a little bit, I found out that some trial had come and his seemingly strong, contagious faith in God, like smoke, had vanished.

> And the ones on the rock are those who, when they hear the word, receive it with joy. But these have no root; they believe for a while, and in time of testing fall away.

Why does this seed die? Because there is no water and no room for the seed to grow, so there is no root; in times of testing, they fall away. You see, it is possible to find the message of Jesus appealing, to be caught up in the emotion of dynamic worship, to be captivated by powerful preaching and to even respond with a prayer to Jesus at the altar call (I see that hand!) . . . and yet still be the rocky soil. Are you the rocky soil?

The Thorny Soil

This is the kind of person who hears and receives the seed of the word of God, but rather than the seed taking over his or her life, it becomes just a part of that person's life. In the gospels there's a story about a rich young guy wanting to get some religion from Jesus. He wants to know from Jesus what he *must do* to be saved. Jesus, knowing this man's heart is not broken as it needs to be (since he believes there's something he "must do" to be saved) drives him to the commandments. "You shall not murder. You shall not commit adultery. You shall not steal. You shall not bear false witness. Honor your father and mother. You shall love your neighbor as yourself."

Now, let's just assume for a moment that this rich young guy has not heard Jesus's teaching that if one is unjustly angry at one's brother it's the same as murder in God's eyes. Let's assume the same thing about the lust and adultery equation that Jesus makes in the Sermon on the Mount. And let's even assume that this young man has never stolen anything or ever told a lie (for sure he had, but for the sake of argument). You would think that the last two commands listed, "Honoring parents" and "Loving your neighbor as yourself" perfectly would force him to admit that at some point he hadn't done it and therefore he didn't make the cut. But *no sir*! This young man simply responds in the most nonchalant of ways, "All these I have kept. What do I still lack?"

Well—Jesus knows this kid can't go on believing these lies about himself. He knows that this guy wants God as an add-on to his life, not the ruler over all his life. So he gives him one of the most difficult words in all of the gospels, "Okay fine. You think you've obeyed me perfectly? You think you're crushing it huh? If you would be perfect, go, sell what you possess, and give to the poor, and you will have treasure in heaven; and come, follow me." With this one command, the man's illusions about himself melt away. Suddenly he is forced to recognize that he doesn't love his neighbor as himself in the way he thought he did. And he certainly doesn't love God enough to get rid of everything and follow him. In fact, when it came down to it, he loved his possessions more.

When the young man heard this he went away sorrowful, for he had great possessions.

The riches of this present world were the thorns that kept this young man from being able to bear fruit. The thorns are the cares and riches and pleasures of this life; for this soil, the seed is something that is received as a sort of an add on to all the other stuff in their life. This is what thorny soil looks like: Jesus is Lord, but I just need to steal a little bit to pay off some debts. Jesus is Lord, but if I don't lie on my taxes, I won't make it. Jesus is Lord, but my spouse is cold to me and I need the attention that my coworker gives me. Jesus is Lord, but I will never forgive my brother for what he did to me.

Are you the thorny soil?

The Good Soil

Ahh . . . finally, the good soil: the one who hears the word and understands it. In other words, the people who get it. Isn't it nice to "get it," to be on the inside? Isn't it nice to always be soft and receptive to the word of God instead of hard and impenetrable like some people you know? Also, isn't it great to be so deeply rooted in your faith that when trials come, you simply rejoice and let them roll right off your back? And oh man, I'm super glad I'm past being distracted by the cares, riches, and pleasures of this life. No creature comforts for me, thank you very much! I'm so glad I'm me: the good soil who always hears and understands, producing so much fruit the world doesn't have enough room to store it. Aren't you?

Wait, what's that? You still struggle with receiving and believing God's word? You still struggle when trials come your way to believe? Hold up. Are you telling me that you find yourself addicted to your creature comforts? Are you suggesting that you might not always be the good soil?

Okay. Fine. Me too. And here's the deal: we're not alone. In Romans 3:11 it literally says that "no one understands, and no one seeks after God!" But the good soil is literally defined by its ability to understand! I mean if this is true then this is an absolute and utter disaster because it means that none of us are naturally the good soil! And that means in and of ourselves, we are completely incapable of producing a fruitful harvest. Yes, that's precisely what it means. By nature every one of us is the hardened path that refuses to let the word of God penetrate us every day of our lives. By nature we are the rocky soil that is so fickle in our faith. By nature we are the thorny soil when we say, "God can have this, this, and this in my life, but he can't have my money or my addiction or my sex life or you name it." There is none of us in and of ourselves that are good soil and are worthy of judgment.

So then . . . what? The only way we can become good soil is if God by his amazing grace makes us good soil who can hear and understand his word. Here's the good news for us: God is in the business of opening up ears and making people good soil fit for his kingdom. Check this out: Psalm 40:6 says, "In sacrifice and offering you have not delighted, but you have given me an open ear." Or more literally in the Hebrew, "but ears you have dug for me." As he brings you to himself in the waters of baptism, the hardened soil of your soul is softened, the rocks are washed away, and the thorny weeds are uprooted. New ears are being dug for you. As you hear God's word proclaiming that though you're a great sinner, Christ is a greater Savior, new ears are being dug for you. As you hear the proclamation of Jesus's perfect life lived in your place, new ears are being dug for you. As you see him up on the cross, suffering for your sins, new ears are being dug for you. As you hear him proclaim that you are completely righteous and forgiven of all your sins on account of his resurrection from the dead, new ears are being dug for you. And as he ascends to the right hand of the Father in victory over sin, death, and hell, promising to always intercede on your behalf, new ears are being dug for you. This is the amazing truth: the generous spreading of the seed can take the hardest, rockiest, thorniest soil and dig ears in there to make anybody good soil ready to receive his word and bear fruit.

"Good Guys and Bad Guys"

One of those rare ideas that often unites both the quasi-religious and the "super-religious" legalistic folks among us is the idea that ultimately what will save a person is how good he or she is. You ask quasi-religious people how they know they will go to heaven someday and chances are (no matter what belief system they hold to), they will probably give you an answer something like "my good outweighs my bad, so I'm pretty confident God will let me in."

At the same time, you ask super-religious, legalistic people what they need to get into heaven and you'll hear them say something very similar. Yes, it will be couched in spiritual-sounding language, but scratch beneath the surface of the pious words, and it will probably boil down to, "You need to be *really, really good* to get into heaven."

One says you just need to have 51 percent "goodness" compared to 49 percent "badness" and you're in, while the other says you need to have the much higher ratio of let's say 90 percent goodness to 10 percent badness to even think about eternal life. But essentially, they're both using the same scale.

This thinking makes sense, because this is the hallmark of natural man's religion: climb the ladder, be the winner. Work hard enough, earn your spot. Then, along comes our parable, tossing over the scale and screwing the whole thing up:

> He also told this parable to some who trusted in themselves that they were righteous, and treated others with contempt: "Two men went up into the temple to pray, one a Pharisee and the other a tax collector. The Pharisee, standing by himself, prayed thus: 'God, I thank you that I am not like other men, extortioners, unjust, adulterers, or even like this tax collector. I fast twice a week; I give tithes of all that I get.' But the tax collector, standing far off, would not even lift up his eyes to heaven, but beat his breast, saying, 'God, be merciful to me, a sinner!' I tell you, this man went down to his house justified, rather than the other. For everyone who exalts himself will be humbled, but the one who humbles himself will be exalted." (Luke 18:9–14)

The "Good Guy"

If you're like me, chances are you've heard a few sermons on this parable before. But I've got to be honest with you: I take issue with the way this is preached a lot of the time, specifically with the way the Pharisee is presented. Oftentimes (to make the point really stand out) preachers will portray the Pharisee as extreme and terribly irritating in his proclamations. He is loud and verbose and quite cocky in his tone of voice. He is haughty in his appearance and is made to look as villainous as possible. But in real life, villains don't show themselves so obviously.

So, let's just take this character at face value. For all intents and purposes, he really does appear to be a good guy. Instead of loudly boasting about his deeds to the world (as some preachers might make it seem), he is shown "standing by himself" in the temple. In other words, it appears that the words he will mouth are words he keeps between him and

God in prayer. Also, notice that he even begins with what sounds like praise: "God, I thank you . . ." So far so good. As this good guy thinks about his life, he praises God for all the sinful lifestyles that he doesn't participate in and for the various ways he's living righteously: "Thank you God that I am not like other men, extortioners, unjust, adulterers, or even like this tax collector. I fast twice a week; I give tithes of all that I get." I don't think this is some sort of show prayer from a caricatured legalist. I think this is the prayer from a man who believes he is praying in a very devout manner. Truth is, in most aspects of his life, this Pharisee probably was "better" than others (at least outwardly). After all, if he really was fasting twice a week and giving tithes of all he received, then he was going above and beyond the call of duty. Indeed, if the Pharisee were alive today, we would certainly recognize him for being an upright man. So what's his problem?

To get the answer, we sort of have to read between the lines a little. For starters, it appears this dude is super proud of himself. Yes, he thanks God at the beginning, but look a little closer and you'll notice five times in his short prayer he mentions the word *I*. This Pharisee was completely focused on himself and all that *he* had done. His prayer to God was really just a facade for praying to himself. Really, he was thanking himself for being different than others. He was doing what we might call today a humble-brag (a statement that sounds humble but is really a secret way of bragging). Chances are you've done this yourself and certainly have heard others do it.

As a pastor, I can attest that my fellow clergymen and I fall into this trap all the time. It might sound something like this: "I thank God that since I arrived at this church, we've grown by leaps and bounds. I'm really praising God for all the programs I've been able to initiate and for all the new faces I—oops, I mean God has brought in . . ."

But the biggest problem with the Pharisee's prayer is that he judges himself compared to other people, rather than to God. Our natural tendency is to do just this. I mean we can all think of people that we're better than: "Sure, I'm not perfect, but it's not like I'm as bad as _____." Once we do that, it's only a small leap to move to, "Therefore, I'm doing okay." And if we've deemed ourselves okay, then we're pretty sure God will too.

Shortly after leaving his office as mayor, Michael Bloomberg was interviewed about his work. In his mind, because of all his work fighting obesity, smoking cessation and gun control, with a grin to the interviewer he said: "I am telling you if there is a God, when I get to heaven I'm not stopping to be interviewed. I am heading straight in. I have earned my place in heaven. It's not even close."[1]

Contrary to what Bloomberg (and this Pharisee) thinks, our good deeds are not what will grant us entrance into heaven. You may do a lot of nice things and you may be a really generous person. You may have paid your taxes on time, and hey, maybe you were even so good that you were the one guy who actually checked that little box to give a little extra to the government, but I'm telling you, the Bible is telling you, before God none of that stuff is gonna cut it. God does not grade on a curve.

The Bible says no one is righteous enough, not one (Rom. 3:10). The Bible declares that from birth we are infected and plagued with a sinful nature and by nature are at war with God. Even worse news, it declares that there is no way of making up for this problem. We cannot become redeemable in it of ourselves. We are by nature damned.

But our Pharisee is blinded by the comparison game. His prayer would sound quite a bit different if his comparison was to the standards of a holy and just God. But yeah, sure, if you compare yourself to a tax collector you just might convince yourself. Of course you're better than him!

Frankly, everyone in that society was pretty sure they were better than him.

The Bad Guy

Just as we must avoid a caricature of the Pharisee, we must also avoid the caricature of the tax collector. We have to stop and give a little background to this man before we plunge forward. Tax collectors were some of the most despised people in all of Jewish life. And there was a good reason for their being despised.

The tax collector was a Jew who had essentially traded sides and was working for the Roman occupiers rather than with the Jews. They were seen as collaborators with the enemy. They charged extra to their countrymen and got rich doing so. So hated were they that they were sometimes referred to by the simple title, "Sinner." So we must not whitewash where this tax collector was coming from. He was probably a bad guy who had done wrong and treated his own people poorly. And yet, to the audience's surprise, he headed to the temple to pray.

What happened to make this sinful man feel like he should go to the temple? We can be fairly certain that this wasn't a regular visit for him but rather something unique for him. Yet here he was heading to the temple to fellowship with God when Jesus gives us an interesting detail: he "was standing far off." Did he get to the temple and feel that he was just so unholy that he had no right to enter with the rest of the people? Did he think that others would look down on him in church if he went in like the rest of them? Was he just sure if he darkened the doors of the church he'd burst into flames? We don't know. All we know is that this tax collector stands far off from the rest. He knows he doesn't belong with the rest of these good church people. After all, he's a bad guy.

Maybe some of you reading this now have felt like that about going to church? Your addiction, your sexuality, your theft, your_____ has left you believing that there's just no place for you there.

I remember reading this passage out of Philip Yancey's book *What's So Amazing About Grace?* some years ago, and it hit me like a ton of bricks. A prostitute came to a friend of his in wretched straits, homeless, sick, unable to buy food for her two-year-old daughter. His friend describes the scene:

> Through sobs and tears, she told me she had been renting out her daughter—two years old!—to men . . . for you know what. She made more renting out her daughter for an hour than she could earn on her own in a night. She had to do it, she said, to support her own drug habit. I could hardly bear hearing her sordid story. For one thing, it made me legally liable—I'm required to report cases of child abuse. I had no idea what to say to this woman. At last I asked if she had ever thought of going to a church for help. I will never forget the look of pure, naïve shock that crossed her face. "Church!" she cried. "Why would I ever go there? I was already feeling terrible about myself. They'd just make me feel worse."[2]

The tax collector seems to feel the same way. He is so ashamed of his actions that he can't even look to heaven, beating his breast over and over as he encounters a holy God. He is well aware of his sin, and he has nothing articulate to say. No declarations; no accomplishments to boast of; just a heartfelt plea: "God, be merciful to me, a sinner!"

In the Greek, the sentence he says could be rendered, "O God, be propitiated toward me, *the* sinner." Notice, there's no comparison for this man to other people. He refers to himself as "*the sinner*." And as such, he knows God must be propitiated toward him. That is, he senses that a sacrifice must be made to God to appease his wrath at his sin. It is the only way. This tax collector hopes that some way, somehow, the enmity brought by his sin between him and God can be dealt with for him to have any real chance of a right relationship to God. The good news for the tax collector, and us, is that God has indeed provided a propitiation for our sins.

The Justified Guy

First John 2: 2 says about Jesus, "He is the propitiation for our sins, and not for ours only but also for the sins of the whole world." Let that sink in: God has provided propitiation for himself so sinners like this tax collector are completely forgiven and declared wholly righteous. Thus, Jesus can go on to deliver the shocking conclusion to the story: "I tell you, this man went down to his house justified, rather than the other. For everyone who exalts himself will be humbled, but the one who humbles himself will be exalted." Indeed, the only thing that separates the justified and unjustified is not whether they're "good guys" or "bad guys." Rather it is based on whose righteousness they're depending on: their own or Christ's.

I mentioned at the beginning of this chapter that sometimes I get irked by the way the Pharisee is often portrayed. That's not all that irks me (sorry). There's one other thing that usually comes at right about this moment in the sermon as the preacher wraps up. It usually comes in the form of a question, and it goes like this: "So, which one of these characters are you? Are you the humble tax collector or the proud Pharisee?"

Any sane person knows that the answer should obviously be "the humble tax collector." *But* . . . if we're honest, any one of us is a mixture of both on any given day. Sometimes I am utterly humbled by my sin, while at other times, I can be a proud son of a gun. If we're honest, we find ourselves comparing our righteousness to others all the time. As David

Zahl has said, "'All have sinned and fall short of the glory of God,' But that hasn't stopped us from comparing distances."

Each of us stands or kneels as a combination of the two men in our parable. Because as Martin Luther said, we are simultaneously saint and sinner. Nevertheless, the solution to the problem is always the same. Whether we find ourselves becoming too proud of our accomplishments or utterly humbled by our failures, the plea on our lips should always and ever be, "Lord, have mercy on me, the sinner." Amen.

Notes

1   The New York Times, April 15, 2014, Page A12
2   Philip Yancey, *What's So Amazing About Grace?* (Grand Rapids, MI: Zondervan, 1997), 11.

Go Waste Your Righteousness

And behold, a lawyer stood up to put him to the test, saying, "Teacher, what shall I do to inherit eternal life?" He said to him, "What is written in the Law? How do you read it?" And he answered, "You shall love the Lord your God with all your heart and with all your soul and with all your strength and with all your mind, and your neighbor as yourself." And he said to him, "You have answered correctly; do this, and you will live." But he, desiring to justify himself, said to Jesus, "And who is my neighbor?" Jesus replied, "A man was going down from Jerusalem to Jericho, and he fell among robbers, who stripped him and beat him and departed, leaving him half dead. Now by chance a priest was going down that road, and when he saw him he passed by on the other side. So likewise a Levite, when he came to the place and saw him, passed by on the other side. But a Samaritan, as he journeyed, came to where he was, and when he saw him, he had compassion. He went to him and bound up his wounds, pouring on oil and wine. Then he set him on his own animal and brought him to an inn and took care of him. And the next day he took out two denarii and gave them to the innkeeper, saying, 'Take care of him, and whatever more you spend, I will repay you when I come back.' Which of these three, do you think, proved to be a neighbor to the man who fell among the robbers?" He said, "The one who showed him mercy." And Jesus said to him, "You go, and do likewise."

—Luke 10:25–37

Few things are certain in life. Death. Taxes. And when you show too much compassion to sinners, somebody will decide it is necessary to stand up for righteousness. Take it to the bank. It will happen. This happened to Jesus over and over during his three years of earthly ministry. When looking at the parable of the good Samaritan, it's important to remember this is the sort of self-perceived crusader for righteousness Jesus is talking to. All this talk of the kingdom of God coming for the poor, the weak, and the downtrodden must be explained. When this *lawyer (expert in Jewish law) asks the question, "What shall I do to inherit eternal life?" he* does not desire an answer for himself. He is looking for Jesus to tell those around him that they must *do* what this man already believes he is doing. The question is not, "How does one inherit eternal life?" No. He is testing Jesus to see if he will prescribe the correct deeds necessary to please God and receive his blessing. Is this popular teacher from the middle of nowhere going to tell his followers what they must do, or is he just going to keep blessing the weary and heavy-laden? That is the test Jesus has just been put to.

Do I need to tell you putting Jesus to the test is a bad idea? Probably not. Jesus gives the lawyer half the answer he wants but in doing so tosses the question back to him. If you want to find eternal life through what you do or abstain from doing, Jesus will always throw you back to the Law. The lawyer had no trouble answering the question, "What is written in the Law? How do you read it?" He quickly gave the correct answer: love God with your whole being and love your neighbor as yourself. *Boom!* Jesus had him right where he wanted him. He commended him for answering correctly and told him to do that and he would live. This is God's way of saying, "Cool. How are you doing with that whole love God and neighbor perfectly business?"

Apparently, this guy thought he was doing pretty well in the loving God department and equally well in the neighbor department . . . as long as those neighbors were who he thought they were. You must understand this is the same Jesus who earlier in his famous Sermon on the Mount said, "You have heard that it was said, 'You shall love your neighbor and hate your enemy.' But I say to you, Love your enemies and pray for those who persecute you" (Matthew 5:44–45). When Jesus said, "You have heard it said," who was he talking about? This guy and others like him. The teachers and experts in law. Jesus was most certainly hanging around and loving people this lawyer most certainly did not consider his neighbors. This is why instead of walking away, he had to ask the self-justifying question, "Who is my neighbor?"

Self-justifying is a dangerous game to play with God in the flesh. Because he has stories. Scandalous, self-justifying, heart-seeking missile type stories. This is one of them

Samaritan Laws and Who Jesus Is Trying to Offend

When we hear the word *Samaritan*, it doesn't hit our ears the same way it would have hit the ears of Jesus's audience. We name charitable organizations after the nameless good guy in this story. In the area I live in, there are several of them: Samaritan's Purse, Samaritan's House, Samaritan's Food Bank, etc. We even have laws called Good Samaritan laws. These laws protect people from being sued if they try to help someone in a bad situation and it goes poorly. When someone stops and helps you when your car breaks down, you may even refer to that person as a Good Samaritan. For us all the connotations connected with the word *Samaritan* are good. A Samaritan is selfless, charitable, and sacrificial. It's a title none of us would mind being associated with. However, none of that was the case for Jesus's audience.

Samaritans had heretical worship practices, and Samaria was a haven for Jewish outlaws and fugitives. We see in the story of Jesus and the Samaritan woman at the well that Jews and Samaritans didn't interact with one another.

> The Samaritan woman said to him, "How is it that you, a Jew, ask for a drink from me, a woman of Samaria?" (For Jews have no dealings with Samaritans.) (John 4:9)

Jesus was undoubtedly out to offend to the confident religious leader, but he was also seeking to scandalize his own disciples. In the previous chapter, the disciples of Jesus had an encounter with Samaritans.

> When the days drew near for him to be taken up, he set his face to go to Jerusalem. And he sent messengers ahead of him, who went and entered a village of the Samaritans, to make preparations for him. But the people did not receive him, because his face was set toward Jerusalem. And when his disciples James and John saw it, they said, "Lord, do you want us to tell fire to come down from heaven and consume them?" But he turned and rebuked them. And they went on to another village. (Luke 9:51–55)

Because of this, I believe the parable is not only for the one questioning Jesus but also for the self-righteous disciples who right before this thought their Rabbi would approve of the destruction of a Samaritan town Sodom and Gomorrah style. Perhaps you can see the very fact that we refer to this parable as "The Good Samaritan" shows us just how scandalous this story really is. Samaritans don't get the role of the "good guy" in this culture. But a whole lot goes down in this story before the heretical hero enters in the form of the despised Samaritan.

The Way of Blood

If you grew up in church, you are probably familiar with what happens when someone stops going. I'm not talking about when someone changes churches. I'm talking about when someone leaves the church altogether. The lines between concern and gossip get blurry fast. If the far-too-popular phrase "walk with God" means anything, it at least exists to contrast those on the right path and those on the wrong one. "Stay in church and close to God and everything will go well, but if you're out there running around with the world, don't be surprised if bad things happen." At least that is the way we typically hear it.

> A man was going down from Jerusalem to Jericho, and he fell among robbers, who stripped him and beat him and departed, leaving him half dead.

The road Jesus is referring to was well known. It was given the name "The Way of Blood" due to being notoriously dangerous and occupied by violent robbers. Jerusalem was the city of God. It's where the temple was. It's where the people of God gathered. Those listening to this story are already thinking: *If you're going down from Jerusalem, don't be surprised if something bad happens. Don't be where you know you shouldn't be. Stay close to the church. I see where the moral of this story is headed. Who is my neighbor? Those who stay where they're supposed to be.*

Rethinking the Robber

There is a surface-level application to this parable that is pretty obvious. If you come across someone robbed and beat half to death, you should help them. I can think of very few people (Christian or not) who would argue against such an ethic. It's basic *golden rule* stuff. And while it's easy to affirm, it's anything but easy to practice. Especially when you get more details. And Jesus is giving details.

Desperate men are not the only thieves and murders among us. There is a scene in the 2003 movie *Luther* where a young boy commits suicide. According to the Roman church, suicide was a mortal sin, and he was condemned to hell. Then Martin Luther makes a profound statement:

> Some say, that according to God's justice this boy is damned because he took his own life. I say he was overcome by the devil. Is this child any more to blame for the despair that overtook him, than an innocent man who was murdered by a robber in the woods?

Jesus says Satan has been "a murderer from the beginning" (John 8:44) and a "thief" who "comes only to steal and kill and destroy" (John 10:10). What if the man who went down from Jerusalem on a dangerous road isn't just the equivalent of getting jumped in a dark alley? What if it's that and a whole lot more? I believe it is. I believe it's about those people who are traveling the dangerous road of life in the wrong direction. People warned them. They knew better but did it anyway. And there is murderous robber out there who has beaten them and left them for dead. And by "them" I mean *all of us*.

Head-on Collisions, Blood, and Sin

Why don't the Levite and the priest help this stranger on the road, and why is Jesus so specific about who they were? Priests and Levites are not just Jews but ceremonially clean Jews. They were the men of the cloth of their day. One may think that if anyone would help, it would be these guys. But it's dangerous and expensive. Why are these men even on this perilous road? What are they doing so far from safety and Jerusalem? To help this man will mean they will run several risks: 1. If they don't want others to know where they have been, helping could expose that. 2. Helping takes time, and obviously this isn't a safe place to spend a few hours. 3. This guy is a bloody mess. He looks dead. If they investigate, and it turns out he is in fact dead, they will become unclean from the corpse. The price tag is too high. So they stay as far away as possible.

Years ago, I was the first person on the scene of a head-on collision. It was horrific. I rushed from my car to help. One driver was already dead, and the other was unconscious, with the dashboard of his truck caved in against his chest, pinning him in the vehicle. There was a woman in the passenger seat. She was in a swimsuit and had cuts all over her body. She was screaming in total shock. I couldn't get her door open, so I cleared out the glass from the shattered window and pulled her through the opening. I carried her a little way from the wreck and set her in the grass and then called the 911. Only after the first responders arrived and I was free to go, did I realize that the white shirt I was wearing was covered in the woman's blood, as were my arms and neck.

There is nothing special about the way I responded. I believe anyone would respond that way. But after it was over, there was no denying I had just been involved in something horrific. The evidence of disaster was all over me. Now imagine that isn't blood . . . it's sin. Neither the priest or the Levite were willing to risk getting spiritually dirty.

At this point in the story, Jesus wasn't telling the questioning lawyer or the angry disciples who their neighbors were or how they should love them. Not yet. Jesus was telling them who they were. He is telling us who we are. We are all simultaneously the nameless man left for dead on a dangerous path away from God and the priest and Levite unwilling to dirty ourselves with others who have been overcome by sin and the devil's murderous work. We aren't pulling anyone out of spiritual head-on collisions; we were driving the car.

The Good and Despised Samaritan

> But a Samaritan, as he journeyed, came to where he was, and when he saw him, he had compassion. He went to him and bound up his wounds, pouring on oil and wine. Then he set him on his own animal and brought him to an inn and took care of him. And the next day he took out two denarii and gave them to the innkeeper, saying, 'Take care of him, and whatever more you spend, I will repay you when I come back.

Sin has left all of us for dead on the dangerous road away from God. But God himself will travel that road to rescue, mend, and save us. He doesn't show up as a glorious and powerful king. He appears as one rejected and despised. He will be accused of all kinds of heresy. He will be opposed for the fugitives he harbors. He will show up like a Samaritan. He isn't afraid to travel the Way of Blood. He journeys that road seeking and saving the lost, miserable, and dead. He counts all of humanity as his neighbors. He comes to us overwhelmed with compassion, and without us asking, he binds our wounds and carries us to the inn of the church.

He pays for everything with his blood and promises to return for all he has rescued. Jesus is the only good and despised Samaritan.

Jesus is the hero of his own parable, but he has cast the most unlikely person to play his part. He was someone who scandalized both the religious leaders and his own disciples. It serves as a prophetic word that he will be spurned and rejected by his own people, but people of every background and unsavory reputation will be brought into his kingdom.

So, You Want to Be Like Jesus?

Jesus concluded his story by saying "You go, and do likewise." This is the part we are prone to focus on. We see it as an admonition to go be good and helpful people. But it's more than that. It must be heard in light of the whole story. As we "go," there are things we must we come to grips with if we want to be little Christs to a world left for dead.

Go and know you were dying apart from God, beaten by sin, and without aid or hope.

Go and know a despised and rejected God brought you back to life when all others passed you by.

Go and know that in his compassion, he has paid for all things necessary for you to live and has promised to return for you at an appointed time.

Go and know that to love your neighbor is messy and involves wasting your perceived righteousness and reputation. It means walking the Way of Blood.

Go and know that there is only one truly good Samaritan, and he goes with you.

Who Is Your Father?

Now the tax collectors and sinners were all drawing near to hear him. And the Pharisees and the scribes grumbled, saying, "This man receives sinners and eats with them." And he said, "There was a man who had two sons. And the younger of them said to his father, 'Father, give me the share of property that is coming to me.' And he divided his property between them. Not many days later, the younger son gathered all he had and took a journey into a far country, and there he squandered his property in reckless living. And when he had spent everything, a severe famine arose in that country, and he began to be in need. So he went and hired himself out to one of the citizens of that country, who sent him into his fields to feed pigs. And he was longing to be fed with the pods that the pigs ate, and no one gave him anything. But when he came to himself, he said, 'How many of my father's hired servants have more than enough bread, but I perish here with hunger! I will arise and go to my father, and I will say to him, "Father, I have sinned against heaven and before you. I am no longer worthy to be called your son. Treat me as one of your hired servants."' And he arose and came to his father. But while he was still a long way off, his father saw him and felt compassion, and ran and embraced him and kissed him. And the son said to him, 'Father, I have sinned against heaven and before you. I am no longer worthy to be called your son.' But the father said to his servants, 'Bring quickly the best robe, and put it on him, and put a ring on his hand, and shoes on his feet. And bring the fattened calf and kill it, and let us eat and celebrate. For this my son was dead, and is alive again; he was lost, and is found.' And they began to celebrate. Now his older son was in the field, and as he came and drew near to the house, he heard music and dancing. And he called one of the servants and asked what these things meant. And he said to him, 'Your brother has come, and your father has killed the fattened calf, because he has received him back safe and sound.' But he was angry and refused to go in. His father came out and entreated him, but he answered his father, 'Look, these many years I have served you, and I never disobeyed your command, yet you never gave me a young goat, that I might celebrate with my friends. But when this son of yours came, who has devoured your property with prostitutes, you killed the fattened calf for him!' And he said to him, 'Son, you are always with me, and all that is mine is yours. It was fitting to celebrate and be glad, for this your brother was dead, and is alive; he was lost, and is found.'" (Luke 15:1–2, 11–32)

It seems when God came here in the flesh there were always two groups of people that hung out near him. The first group were generally outcasts, sick people, weirdos, drunks, prostitutes, tax collectors, thieves, murderers, adulterers, and other deplorables best known as "sinners." But there was another group that was always lurking near Jesus too, and they were the really religious types. The scribes (those who made a living out of copying the law word for word), the Pharisees (the conservative, proudly orthodox strand of Judaism), the Sadducees (what we might think of as the more progressive, liberal arm of Judaism), and various other strict moralists found themselves constantly intrigued by Jesus.

Yet in our story today, we find that only one of these groups is "drawing near to Jesus"—the "sinners." They didn't just overhear Jesus, but they came near Jesus. Something about him made them feel welcome enough, comfortable enough to come near. This group of losers really was drawn to him, because of him, throughout his whole ministry.

On the other hand, we're told that the second group, the really moral, law-abiding religious folks, couldn't stand being near Jesus and didn't like the fact that he would stand near "such sinners." Oh they were close in proximity to him, but they never could "draw near" to him. So they grumbled: "This man receives sinners and eats with them." The implication is, "This man doesn't take sin seriously enough. He's endorsing their lifestyle. How can he possibly claim to be God in the flesh, the Holy One, and yet let such unclean people draw near!" It is in answer to this objection, speaking to these two groups, Jesus tells this parable.

The Unrighteous Brother

And he said, "There was a man who had two sons. And the younger of them said to his father, 'Father, give me the share of property that is coming to me.'" Now at first upon reading just those words, without knowing the rest of the story, we might be tempted to pass over them quickly. What we may assume from the picture we are given of this younger son is that he seems to be probably typical of many a young person just growing up in their parents' house. He wants to get out and see the world. He doesn't want to live under the rules of his father's house. Besides he sees his friends all around him, moving out, and finally being free from the shackles of living at home. So we may say, "Ahh, typical young man, looking for a little freedom. No harm, no foul." But our assumptions would be wrong about this boy. You see at that time, his request was unheard of. Because in that day, you never asked for the share of your father's inheritance. Ever! The way it worked is generally upon the father's death, the firstborn son would get two-thirds of the father's estate, while the remaining third would go to the younger brother. But this only was supposed to happen at the father's death. So do you see what he's telling his father? In that culture it was seen as a way of telling your dad, "I don't care if you die; I just want your money." This may be why in the next verse, when we read that the Father "divides his property" between his boys, the word for property is actually the word in Greek for "life" (*Bion*). The Father in doing what the younger son is asking him to do is figuratively "dividing his life away."

And so we see that part of what it means to be lost is a desire for the father's things, but not the father himself. It is a belief that you know better than God what's good for you. This is what Satan played on in the garden of Eden with Adam and Eve. Here God, their loving Father, had given our first parents one rule: "Do not eat from the tree of the knowledge of good and evil, but all else in here is yours for your rich enjoyment." What was the devil's ploy? "You will not surely die. For God knows that when you eat of it your eyes will be opened, and you will be like God, knowing good and evil" (Genesis 3:4–5). The implication: "Your dad's holding something back from you—real life! He just doesn't want you to have all that he has."

At this point in the story, Jesus's hearers might expect him to say that the father punished his young son for such a dishonorable request. Or at least maybe the older brother, or the rest of the community. But strangely, we don't hear that any of that happens. Rather, the father, knowing that his son is making a terrible mistake and will get into all sorts of trouble with his share of the inheritance money, allows him to take it anyway.

Our Father will not restrain us forever. Interestingly, Romans 1:24–31 tells us that part of God's judgment of us as sinners and rebels is not necessarily fire from the sky. No, most often he actually just allows us to do what we want (because we refuse and reject him, he "gives us over," Romans 1 says). And don't mistake this "giving over" to necessarily be painful (at least not at first).

At first with all his money, he is having a blast! He is winning friends and influencing people. He has moved into a sweet studio apartment in SoHo, is hosting parties, and is hooking up with beautiful women. At this point he can't see any reason why he'd ever want to move home again. As Hebrews 11 confirms for us, "sin can indeed be pleasurable" . . . for a season. And at this moment, the partying, the sex, and the fun seem *great*!

Nevertheless, the tide turns quickly because the very next verse tells us,

> When he had spent everything, a severe famine arose in that country, and he began to be in need. So he went and hired himself out to one of the citizens of that country, who sent him into his fields to feed pigs. And he was longing to be fed with the pods that the pigs ate, and no one gave him anything.

How fleeting are the pleasures of sin! One day you're on top of the world, and the next you're scraping the bottom of the barrel. He is in a foreign country, and as a Jewish boy, is now doing the most menial, disgusting, unclean work a Jew can do: feeding pigs. Even worse, he's so low, he longs to be fed with their slop!

This is always where sin leads us. It lures us in with promises of freedom and beauty and prestige and then leaves us longing for pig slop. That's what happens to drug addicts, that's what happens to white collar thieves like Bernie Madoff, and that's what happens to people that cheat on their spouses. They don't just wake up one day and say, "I want to destroy my life and the lives of others." No, it starts with just wanting the feeling the drug gives you a little more; it starts with just needing a little more money to "get by." It starts with just wanting a little more attention than you're feeling at home. And then the pig slop comes.

If the story ended right here, there would be a part of us that would feel satisfied. It would be a nice Aesop fable, a moral tale. But like the rest of the Bible, this isn't a morality tale. This is a story of grace, and the story is not over . . . Suddenly, at the bottom, the younger brother remembers his father. Maybe, just maybe his father will take him back, just as a servant. He knows he's forfeited his rights as a son, but maybe his father will take him back as a worker. Anything is better than this! And so the younger son does what I guess anyone who's almost broken would do in this situation: he rehearses a speech.

> Father, I have sinned against heaven and before you. I am no longer worthy to be called your son. Treat me as one of your hired servants.

Can't you see him repeating this over and over as he makes his way back to his home? What will his father say? Will his father even acknowledge him? With each step those questions become more and more nerve-inducing. In that culture, everything was based on honor. For what this youngest son did, surely any self-respecting father would not have anything to do with this son ever again, as he would have seen his son as dead to him. By this time, his Father's house was just around the bend. His stomach was in knots, and he was sweating profusely.

As the son turned the bend, rehearsing his speech, to his absolute shock "while he was still a long way off, his father saw him and felt compassion, and ran and embraced him and kissed him." In that culture, a dignified man never ran. A dignified man walked slowly in his long, flowing robes. But this father was so overwhelmed with compassion for his son that it was as if all thought of what others thought of him went out the window. All that mattered now was that his son was home, so he lifted his robe off the ground and ran out to his son, showering him with hugs and kisses.

"Bring quickly the best robe, and put it on him, and put a ring on his hand, and shoes on his feet," the father yelled. "Bring the fattened calf and kill it and let us eat and celebrate," said the jubilant father.

So what does all this have to do with you? Everything. Because a part of every one of us is this son. We, through our sinful tendencies, have abandoned God a thousand times, and yet, the message to you who have run off to a far country is you are always welcomed home. And here's why: because just as the father divided his property, his life, Jesus divided his life, his everything for you, even when you would squander it away. Because of this sacrifice, this absorption of sin and wrongdoing done to him, he has covered your nakedness, your sin before God with the best robe. "For as many of you as were baptized into Christ have put on Christ" (or been clothed in Christ) the apostle Paul tells us (Galatians 3:27). In Christ Jesus you have been given the signet ring. When one wore this ring, one was given the right to sign in the father's name again. It was a symbol of being a son. Though slaves and servants would not have worn shoes, this is the father's son. Sons wear shoes! We have, as Ephesians says, because of Christ, "shoes for our feet, having put on the readiness given by the gospel of peace." And so our Father lavishes his sons and daughters, you and I, with the full declaration that we have complete restoration: "For this my son was dead, and is alive again; he was lost, and is found." And now all that's left is to feast together, to celebrate! Right?

Well . . . Unfortunately, not everyone in this world is happy when grace is handed out so abundantly.

The Self-Righteous Brother

You remember him, right? He heard the news about his brother's homecoming, and far from being happy and celebrating, this guy was furious and refused to go into the party. To tell you the truth, it's understandable why the older brother is angry, isn't it? I mean, the last time he saw his younger brother, he was virtually spitting in his dad's face! Now he was eating the fattened calf (a major delicacy only reserved for the most special of occasions!), and without batting an eyelash, the whole community was celebrating right along with him. Meanwhile (at least in his mind) this older brother had served his father in the field faithfully. No wild living for him. He'd never left home. He'd never squandered his father's belongings! He'd done what he'd been told! No, *hell no*, he was not going to celebrate his younger brother's return.

It's important to remember at this point who Jesus is telling this story to. There were "sinners" and "Pharisees." The "sinners" are clearly represented by the younger brother. Therefore, the older brother must be the Pharisees, the religious types.

You see, contrary to what we might naturally think, it's entirely possible to be very religious and be far from God (maybe even further from God than the nonreligious). This attitude can all too easily slip into the church. Here's how it happens. If you think, *Okay, Jesus got me into a good relationship with the Father when he saved me, but it's up to me to keep God happy, to become more Christlike, to be more righteous to ensure he stays happy*, I can assure you that you will become just like this older brother. Grace will inevitably be an affront to you.

And yet, because the Father loves both of his sons, he comes out to where both of them are at—the younger one off in the distance, and now the older one outside of the party.

And the Father entreats him: "Come inside. I want you to be a part of this celebration too!" But the older brother, this Pharisee, doubles down, responding, "Look (literally 'look you') these many years I have served you (literally 'slaved away' for you, revealing his true feelings about how he felt serving his father), and I never disobeyed your command (oh really?), yet you never gave me a young goat, that I might celebrate with my friends." Look at how self-deluded the religious older brother is: "I have served you, and I *never* disobeyed your command . . ." And notice what was he really serving his father for? "A young goat." The rewards, the benis. He's not so different than his younger brother after all. He's just going about it in a more dignified way. He continues his passionate plea for justice: "But when this son of yours came, who has devoured your property with prostitutes, you killed the fattened calf for him!" Translation: "Don't you see how bad he was! I'm better, I'm better! I'm better!"

So which brother are you? Are you the unrighteous or the self-righteous? The younger or the older? Here's the answer: you're both. You have sinned and gone off to a far country, but you have also sinned in believing you're more righteous than others.

The Righteous Brother

And yet, the father invites both brothers in; the younger comes in, but we never hear what the older does. Unfortunately, we find out from the rest of the Jesus's story most of the older brothers never really came around: The older brothers in Jesus's story ended up having the Father arrested, tried, whipped, beaten, and crucified. They rejected the Father's invitation, but you don't have to. His invitation to come in and rejoice with him still stands. Because a sacrifice has been made—the sacrifice of another brother, a truly righteous brother. That sacrifice is there for you to feast on today, and it is so much better than a fatted calf. The feast he invites you to partake in is the feast of his very own body and blood for the covering of your sins. He invites the older brothers and younger brothers to his feast today. To all, the Father says, "Come." Repent of your self-righteousness, repent of your unrighteousness, and enjoy the feast that the Father has provided for younger brothers, for older brothers, for you.

A Dangerous World for Sinners

Then Peter came up and said to him, "Lord, how often will my brother sin against me, and I forgive him? As many as seven times?" Jesus said to him, "I do not say to you seven times, but seventy-seven times. 'Therefore the kingdom of heaven may be compared to a king who wished to settle accounts with his servants. When he began to settle, one was brought to him who owed him ten thousand talents. And since he could not pay, his master ordered him to be sold, with his wife and children and all that he had, and payment to be made. So the servant fell on his knees, imploring him, "Have patience with me, and I will pay you everything." And out of pity for him, the master of that servant released him and forgave him the debt. But when that same servant went out, he found one of his fellow servants who owed him a hundred denarii, and seizing him, he began to choke him, saying, "Pay what you owe." So his fellow servant fell down and pleaded with him, "Have patience with me, and I will pay you." He refused and went and put him in prison until he should pay the debt. When his fellow servants saw what had taken place, they were greatly distressed, and they went and reported to their master all that had taken place. Then his master summoned him and said to him, "You wicked servant! I forgave you all that debt because you pleaded with me. And should not you have had mercy on your fellow servant, as I had mercy on you?" And in anger his master delivered him to the jailers, until he should pay all his debt.'" (Matthew 18:21–34)

Many of the rabbis in Jesus's day taught that you had to forgive someone three times—a sort of three strikes and you're out rule. Peter had been hanging out with Jesus for a while now. He seemed to understand that Jesus was quite a bit more gracious than the religious leaders. He presented an option to Jesus that was more than double what was commonly required. Seven times seems very generous. Perhaps Jesus would give him a pat on the back, saying, "You're really starting to understand this whole kingdom of God thing, Peter." But that's not even close to how extravagantly Jesus views forgiveness. Seventy-seven times is just a clever way of saying forgiveness has no limits. It keeps going and going. He tells this story to illustrate that we understand neither the enormity of God's forgiveness nor the danger of our unforgiveness.

Getting More Than We Asked For

The debt of the first man in this story is something no servant could ever hope to repay. It's difficult to imagine how a servant could even acquire such an enormous debt. It's purposely absurd. And it makes the man's plea—"Have patience with me, and I will pay you everything"—utterly preposterous. No amount of patience on the king's part is going to get this debt paid.

The patience of God is well documented in the pages of the Bible. Over and over again God is described as being "slow to anger." That is a very good thing. Humanity has given God no shortage of things to be angry about. But even a snail eventually gets to its destination. Like this man, we believe if we are given enough time, we can work our way out of the situation we've put ourselves in and back into the good graces of God. But that isn't how this works. We need mercy.

Mercy is what we need when we learn patience isn't going to be enough. Like this man, we are too confident in our own abilities to ask for it. In the midst of our promises to make everything right, a flood of pity washes over the heart of God. Pity is the right word. Sinners making promises to God they could hope to keep—it's a pitiful scene indeed. The divine pity of God produces mercy we weren't asking for. Right in the middle of begging for more time to make everything right, we hear that all is forgiven. God is interrupting our ridiculous appeals with a word of absolution and sending us on our way. We are free . . . but we're not good at it.

Mercy Amnesia

It's easy to understand the anger of the fellow servants when this guy who was forgiven an impossible debt went out and grabbed their friend by the throat and demanded he pay him back a much smaller one. What kind of person does that? How bad do you have to be to so quickly forget the surprise absolution you just received? Perhaps this man believed forgiveness from king to servant was different. The king has so much, and we have so little. We cannot afford to let debts go unpaid the way he can. Or maybe his line of thought was, *Of course I cannot pay such a massive debt, but this smaller debt is reasonable and ought to be paid. If this were all I owed the king, I certainly would have paid it!* Whatever was going through his heart in this moment, it is certain that the recent terror of being condemned followed by the reception of unexpected mercy had left it.

The king believed that mercy ought to produce mercy. He believed mercy should trample over sin in a stampede of underserved absolution. This wicked servant was neither patient nor merciful. When he asked for patience, he received mercy. When his fellow servant asked for patience, he received a debtor's prison sentence. At the end of divine patience is righteous anger. And it seems unforgiveness is the quickest road between them. It angers God because he desires a world where trespass is overcome by grace. Right before Saint James's famous "faith without works is dead" statement, he writes, "Judgment is without mercy to one who has shown no mercy. Mercy triumphs over judgment" (James 2:13). It is faith without mercy that is dead. This faith has forgotten the dire circumstances in which it was conceived. This is a faith that doesn't believe it's really forgiven. It believes the king will someday still demand payment, so it begins collecting from its debtors. It grabs fellow sinners by the throat and chokes out their pitiful pleas. Jesus is letting us know the kingdom of God makes war on debt and judgment and defeats it with mercy and absolution.

Find a Preacher, Lest You Forget

We might identify with the anger of the fellow servants, but this parable is telling us that we all are prone to forget about the mercy we received. I know I am. I have had the honor of speaking in a lot of different churches over the last few years. The most common response I receive after preaching that we are all great sinners, but God is a greater Savior, is some version of, "It's so good to hear that message again. We all need to be reminded."

The Psalms are full of this reminding. They read like a history of God's grace, forgiveness, and salvation put to song. They talk about sin and the law of God. They recount God's faithfulness to his promises. They call back to mind who we are and what God has done to deliver us. This is one of the primary reasons we need to be preached to. We need someone to expose us for the rotten and wretched servants we are, and then to proclaim to us the mercy and grace of the good King.

Reminding us of and reapplying the mercy we have received is how God makes us merciful. At the institution of the Lord's Supper, Jesus said, "This is my body, which is given for you. Do this in remembrance of me" (Luke 22:19). He is calling us to remember that we are recipients of his mercy, grace, and forgiveness. He institutes a meal to put this forgiveness in our mouths over and over again. A faith that is fed a steady diet of the grace and mercy of God in the body and blood of his Son cannot be dead.

The wicked servant had a problem. He had no preacher. He had no one reminding him of who he was. He had no one continually heralding the good news that he had been forgiven. He had no means of grace. Unbelief took over as judgment flowed from his heart, hands, and tongue. The problem was not that the king didn't tell him to go and be merciful. It wasn't the lack of instruction. The king knew that only mercy begets mercy. The problem was the wicked servant was not reminded of that mercy. The problem is that forgiven sinners are forgetful.

Judge Not . . .

If you have spent any time on social media over the past few years, you may have noticed that John 3:16 has been dethroned as the most-quoted verse in the Bible. That title now belongs to Matthew 7:1, where Jesus says, "Judge not, that you be not judged." Because non-Christians are fond of throwing these words of Jesus in the face of critical believers, there tends to be a lot of effort by Christians to explain how these words don't mean what they seem. I think we can take them at face value, and this parable of the unforgiving servant are those famous words of Jesus in the form of a story.

> Judge not, that you be not judged. For with the judgment
> you pronounce you will be judged, and with the measure
> you use it will be measured to you. (Matthew 7:1–2)

Jesus is trying to protect us from creating a world of ruthless judgment—the kind of world where the best construction is never applied to a person, circumstance, or sin. This happens when we do not believe that mercy triumphs over judgment—when we doubt that grace and forgiveness are more powerful than sin and retribution. As we contribute to this atmosphere of judgment, we help create a world we cannot survive in—a world too dangerous for sinners to inhabit. With every measure of judgment we dish out, our peril increases. No sinner will escape it. Slip up and your fellow servants are sure to rat you out to someone with the power to punish.

Judgment is the enemy of faith because faith is delivered and sustained through grace. As we judge and demand payment from one another, we fashion a world not only skeptical of forgiveness, grace, and mercy but also downright opposed to it. Jesus is telling us a story about what happens when forgetful sinners demand justice. Judge not lest you construct a machine out to destroy the very essence of the kingdom of God. That essence is faith, grace, mercy, and forgiveness.

Forgiveness and Cell Doors

Forgiveness involves the absorption of a wrong. It is to release someone of a debt genuinely owed. For this reason, forgiveness can actually feel wrong. It seems like you're letting someone get away with something you shouldn't. The words *I forgive you* sound like keys unlocking the door of a prison cell justice says should remain locked forever. They should sound like that. That is what those words are. But they open more than one cell door.

The late Corrie Ten Boom and her sister spent ten months in a Nazi concentration camp for hiding Jews during World War II. Her sister died there fifteen days before Corrie's release. Her book *The Hiding Place* is one of the most otherworldly examples of forgiveness I have ever read. In it, she describes her struggle to forgive those responsible for the horrific and inhumane injustices inflicted upon her and her family. When describing this radical forgiveness, she writes, "To forgive is to set a prisoner free, only to discover that prisoner was you."[1]

Corrie Ten Boom discovered that forgiveness and freedom live together. One cannot exist where the other does not. It is no accident that the unforgiving servant ends up in a cell. That is where all unforgiveness takes us in the end. Jesus means for us to be free, and to be free we must be forgiven, and to remain free, we must forgive.

A Christianity Marked by Forgiveness

I fear the reputation of Christians is not one of radical forgiveness. I think it is more likely just the opposite—one of radical judgment. This is a result of forgetting just how much we have been forgiven. We too often concern ourselves with lesser things. The scandalous grace of God is seldom proclaimed from our pulpits. It is the message that in the person and work of Jesus, God has forgiven and justified the ungodly. All debts have been forgiven. All cell doors have been unlocked. When we don't hear this on a regular basis, we forget our absolution and go back to participating in the ruthless judgment of a world trying to justify itself. But all is not lost. The king is sending out preachers. He is calling us to come to his table, and as the bread and wine hit our tongues, he is reminding us that mercy is mightier than judgment and freedom is rooted in forgiveness.

When Jesus teaches us to pray, he includes, "Forgive us our debts, as we also have forgiven our debtors" (Matthew 6:12). He ties all forgiveness together. Forgiveness is a river flowing in a circle. God forgives us, and we forgive others. We forgive others, and God forgives us. This is the radical world God wants us to live in—a world not yet free of sin but free of retribution. A world where judgment is stomped out by mercy.

Note

1   Corrie Ten Boom, *The Hiding Place*. (New York: Bantam Books) 118.

The Divine Guest List

In the 1997 film *The Devil's Advocate*, Keanu Reeves plays an up-and-coming small-town lawyer who's offered a chance to work for a major law firm in the bustling metropolis of New York City. The head of the firm (played by Al Pacino) is an exceptionally charming man who has access to everything the world wants: money, power, sex—you name it, he's got it. As the film progresses, we come to find out that Pacino's character is actually a manifestation of the devil, and of course, his goal is to get as many people to follow him as possible. The movie takes some pretty big theological leaps and of course has a lot of the typical Hollywood problems when addressing spiritual issues, but I think they got at least one thing right: throughout the film, the devil says his favorite sin to tempt people with is vanity.

Indeed, vanity or pride has been used by the devil from the beginning to get us. What was it he lured Adam and Eve with if they ate the forbidden fruit? "Your eyes will be opened and *you'll be like God.*" He doesn't change his tactics much because he knows: 1. this sin of pride will separate us from fellowship with God and 2. by nature all of us want to be sovereign and all we need is a little nudge in that direction to pursue our throne.

In our story, Jesus is dining at the home of a ruler of the Pharisees (pretty important religious guy who probably wore a big religious-looking hat). They have invited him over for the sole purpose of trapping him. They can't stand him, with the fame and adulation he's received; they can't stand him for turning some of their manmade rules upside down; they can't stand him for his compassion to sinners. Ultimately they can't stand him because they're vain and proud. This pride is what keeps them from bowing down to him as their Messiah, and it this pride that ultimately keeps us from bowing down to him as our Lord. So, rather than straight out breathe fire at them and us for our proud hearts, Jesus takes the more subtle approach of telling a couple stories:

> Now he told a parable to those who were invited, when he noticed how they chose the places of honor saying to them, "When you are invited by someone to a wedding feast, do not sit down in a place of honor, lest someone more distinguished than you be invited by him, and he who invited you both will come and say to you, 'Give your place to this person,' and then you will begin with shame to take the lowest place." (Luke 14:7–9)

What's the problem here? Well the problem here is with the guest presuming that he is more honored, more important than he really is. In that day there were actually seats of ranking honor (similar, I suppose, to the head table at a wedding) and this guy presumes that he's so important that he must have a seat with the important people.

We live in a culture that is absolutely infected with this sort of pride of presumption before God. We presume that we're automatically good with God, that we're going to be honored by him. We're near certain that our seat's up at the head of the table. After all, we're pretty good people, (better than most probably, right?), and it's basically a given that God has a spot waiting for me in his heavenly paradise. All dogs go to heaven and stuff. Actually, the Bible says something entirely different. Jesus said in Matthew 7:13–14:

> Enter by the narrow gate. For the gate is wide and the way is easy that leads to destruction, and those who enter by it are many. For the gate is narrow and the way is hard that leads to life, and those who find it are few.

He says a little later on in that same chapter that many will come to him on the day of judgment and say, "Lord, Lord we cast out demons in your name, we performed miracles in your name, etc.," and we're told in what has to be one of the most terrifying passages in all of scripture, Jesus looked at them and said, "Depart from me you workers of lawlessness, I never knew you." (Matt. 7:21–23). Matthew 22:14 says about the kingdom, "Many are called, but few are chosen." Here's the deal about every single one of us: in it of ourselves, apart from his grace, we have no right to expect a seat at the table at all.

The Pharisees presumed that because they were born into the right family that God would look down from heaven, see their DNA and what sterling obedience they had, and be overwhelmed by it. Jesus bursts that bubble emphatically! He says just as at a wedding, you never presume that you're the guest of honor, so too you should not presume any honor before God at all. You come to him with nothing but dishonor. You are entirely dependent on him, the host of the feast, to give you a seat in the first place.

> But when you are invited, go and sit in the lowest place, so that when your host comes he may say to you, 'Friend, move up higher.' Then you will be honored in the presence of all who sit at table with you. For everyone who exalts himself will be humbled, and he who humbles himself will be exalted. (Luke 14:10–11)

But Jesus isn't done hammering these vain religious leaders. He also goes after their need for recognition:

> He said also to the man who had invited him, "When you give a dinner or a banquet, do not invite your friends or your brothers or your relatives or rich neighbors, lest they also invite you in return and you be repaid. But when you give a feast, invite the poor, the crippled, the lame, the blind, and you will be blessed, because they cannot repay you. For you will be repaid at the resurrection of the just." (Luke 14:12–14)

The pride detailed here is the sort of pride that is motivated at least in an underlying way to get name recognition. You invite the popular kids to the party; you provide dinner for those who are well connected, the guys who know a guy, who can get you the good jobs. It's not that you're against giving charity at all. You just want a little attaboy, a little pat on the back if you do. Now it must be said there's certainly nothing wrong with hosting a dinner with bigwigs or well-connected people. That's not Jesus's point here at all. Rather, it's the motivation for why you do what you do. Are you doing what you're doing simply for the pride that comes with recognition and repayment?

Remember again that Jesus is speaking to the Pharisees here. It was them that he was speaking of when he would say at another time,

> Beware of practicing your righteousness before other people in order to be seen by them, for then you will have no reward from your Father who is in heaven. Thus, when you give to the needy, sound no trumpet before you, as the hypocrites do in the synagogues and in the streets, that they may be praised by others. Truly, I say to you, they have received their reward. But when you give to the needy, do not let your

left hand know what your right hand is doing, so that your giving may be in secret. And your Father who sees in secret will reward you. And when you pray, you must not be like the hypocrites. For they love to stand and pray in the synagogues and at the street corners, that they may be seen by others. Truly, I say to you, they have received their reward. But when you pray, go into your room and shut the door and pray to your Father who is in secret. And your Father who sees in secret will reward you. (Matthew 6:1–6)

I know someone who for years has kept a list detailing everyone who has sent a thank-you card to them for the Christmas gift or card they sent out. This person knows exactly who hasn't sent back a thank-you card (making a list and checking it twice). That way, of course, they can tell who's "really grateful" and who's not, right? In contrast, Jesus says,

But when you give a feast, invite the poor, the crippled, the lame, the blind, and you will be blessed, because they cannot repay you. For you will be repaid at the resurrection of the just.

Jesus says, "Whenever you think you're not nicely compensated in this life for your good deed for another person, don't complain about it. Don't expect anything in return. Why are you doing it? For repayment at the resurrection of the just. Your treasure is being built up in heaven."

Well, things are starting to get a little awkward around here. These guys are reading between the lines, and it's clear that Jesus is rebuking them. So I imagine one of them speaks up to try and say something that everyone can uncomfortably agree with and then get back to talking about sports, weather, and other harmless bits of small talk.

> When one of those who reclined at table with him heard these things, he said to him, "Blessed is everyone who will eat bread in the kingdom of God!" (Luke 14:15)

But Jesus will have none of it. Because the fact is, the very kingdom of God the man references is sitting right next to them, but they don't want him. They don't want to eat bread in the kingdom of God if it means eating bread provided by him. So . . .

> He said to him, "A man once gave a great banquet and invited many. And at the time for the banquet he sent his servant to say to those who had been invited, 'Come, for everything is now ready.' But they all alike began to make excuses. The first said to him, 'I have bought a field, and I must go out and see it. Please have me excused.'" (Luke 14:16–18)

You ever told somebody you'd go to their party or event, but then got an opportunity to do something better and just backed out? That's basically what's going on here. In the situation Jesus describes the invitations would have been sent out long before this day, and these guys had already RSVP'ed, saying they'd be there. They said they wanted to dine at the banquet, but when the time came, something else got in the way and owned their hearts. So too when Jesus came on the scene, those who were the most supposedly religious, the Pharisees, were the most condemning and the most pulled away from seeing the kingdom of God revealed in Jesus. They said their greatest desire was to dine with the King, but when the King came and said, "If you've seen me, then you've seen the Father," they picked up stones to stone him.

So there are some reading this right now who say their greatest desire is to dine with the King. Jesus is number one. He's my homeboy, my friend, and I love him with all my heart. But if Jesus were to come back today, right now, and say, "Come, for everything is now ready," would you want to go? What kinds of things do you take more pride in than his kingdom?

The first man Jesus references here takes more pride in his possessions, and his wealth, than he does his seat at the table of the King. He says, "I have bought a field, and I must go out and see it. Please have me excused." Oh Lord, I'll spend time with you later, but look, I gotta take care of my stuff.

> And another said, "I have bought five yoke of oxen, and I go to examine them. Please have me excused." (Luke 14:19)

This man's distracted and takes pride in his work over a seat at the King's table. A feast awaits him; all he has to do is show up! He doesn't have to prepare anything or cook anything; all he has to do is *show up*! But work is calling, and because work is his lord, he will not go. Perhaps some of you reading this are workaholics. I struggle with this myself (even working too much in his name! "O wretched man that I am! Who will deliver me from this body of death? Thanks be to God through Jesus Christ our Lord!" [Rom. 7:24–25]). Jesus says, "Come to me all you who are weary and burdened and I will give you rest," but you say, "I will, Jesus, when I'm done working." Jesus says, "Come, for everything is *now* ready."

The next man maybe gives us the most culturally acceptable and holy-sounding reason for not attending the banquet:

> "I have married a wife, and therefore I cannot come." (Luke 14:20)

"Look, I'm married. I've got a family to take care of here, Lord. I would come with you to feast with you in your eternal kingdom, but family comes first. Besides, I'm pretty sure that there's like a *ton* of Christian radio programs that have taught me this anyway, aren't there?" The Lord says, "Come, for everything is *now* ready." But your family takes precedence over him. You have forgotten the sharp words of Jesus:

> Whoever loves father or mother more than me is not worthy of me, and whoever loves son or daughter more than me is not worthy of me. (Matthew 10:37)

And so the world whom God has spent so much time reaching out to, inviting them with an outstretched arm to come for thousands of years, will seal its fate by rejecting the Son. *But wait*! That's not the end of the story. Thank God, that is not the end of the story. There's good news here. The master will not be thwarted in filling his banquet. He will have a feast one way or another. It's just his banquet, his feast, his kingdom won't look the way we may have expected it to:

> So the servant came and reported these things to his master. Then the master of the house became angry and said to his servant, "Go out quickly to the streets and lanes of the city, and bring in the poor and crippled and blind and lame." And the servant said, "Sir, what you commanded has been done, and still there is room." And the master said to the servant, "Go out to the highways and hedges and compel people to come in, that my house may be filled. For I tell you, none of those men who were invited shall taste my banquet." (Luke 14:21–24)

And in one fell swoop, Jesus Christ turns the whole world upside down. The chosen people, the privileged, the powerful, the (self) righteous, the religious and outwardly pious people will not be the ones that fill his banquet hall.

Rather, God's banquet in the end will be filled with people who've been crippled by their sin, blinded by their shame, and made lame by their guilt. His table will be filled with a bunch of outsiders like the Gentiles of Jesus's day who simply accept his invitation to dine with him. His table will be filled even with the people that reject him now but who eventually come to confess their own pride and vanity that has kept them from him.

The price has already been paid for all to enter in. Jesus has granted you access to the party by his life, death, and resurrection in your place. He says to his Father, "Father, they're with me," and the doors are opened. Before you there is a feast like you can't imagine. Everything's been prepared for you; there's nothing left for you to do. Jesus says, "Come, for everything is now ready." For the broken, the outcast, the sinner, they will have their fill.

The Surprise of the Lambs

"When the Son of Man comes in his glory, and all the angels with him, then he will sit on his glorious throne. Before him will be gathered all the nations, and he will separate people one from another as a shepherd separates the sheep from the goats. And he will place the sheep on his right, but the goats on the left. Then the King will say to those on his right, 'Come, you who are blessed by my Father, inherit the kingdom prepared for you from the foundation of the world. For I was hungry and you gave me food, I was thirsty and you gave me drink, I was a stranger and you welcomed me, I was naked and you clothed me, I was sick and you visited me, I was in prison and you came to me.' Then the righteous will answer him, saying, 'Lord, when did we see you hungry and feed you, or thirsty and give you drink? And when did we see you a stranger and welcome you, or naked and clothe you? And when did we see you sick or in prison and visit you?' And the King will answer them, 'Truly, I say to you, as you did it to one of the least of these my brothers, you did it to me.' Then he will say to those on his left, 'Depart from me, you cursed, into the eternal fire prepared for the devil and his angels. For I was hungry and you gave me no food, I was thirsty and you gave me no drink, I was a stranger and you did not welcome me, naked and you did not clothe me, sick and in prison and you did not visit me.' Then they also will answer, saying, 'Lord, when did we see you hungry or thirsty or a stranger or naked or sick or in prison, and did not minister to you?' Then he will answer them, saying, 'Truly, I say to you, as you did not do it to one of the least of these, you did not do it to me.' And these will go away into eternal punishment, but the righteous into eternal life."

—Matthew 25:31–46

Our Lord is into distinctions. All throughout the gospels, and especially in his parables, you will see distinctions made. There are wise bridesmaids and foolish bridesmaids. There are faithful stewards and lazy stewards. There are wheat and tares. There is good fruit and bad fruit. There are believers and unbelievers, and as our parable shows us, there are sheep and there are goats.

What really separates the sheep from the goats, Christian from non-Christian, heaven from hell?

Let's take a little closer look at our parable to see if we can get an answer:

Doctrine?

Well, surely doctrine is important! I mean, we have to believe the right things about God: that Jesus is the son of God, that he lived, died, and rose again for our sins, that the God revealed in the pages of scripture is true. Yes, all this and more is extremely important. Unlike some out there who would cast aside doctrine because it's seen as divisive, I think it's also just as uniting! And so I think many of us are prone to saying indeed, if there's one thing that separates the sheep and the goats, it might just be that: good, solid, clean doctrine.

But as important as it all is, I have to suggest to you that it may not be ultimately what separates the sheep from the goats. I mean, after all, both groups refer to Jesus with the right title as they stand before him, right? They both call him Lord, which suggests a recognition of who he is, but that does not translate into salvation.

The fact is, it is possible for one to have all the right answers about God (to refer to Jesus as Lord), to have an intellectual understanding of doctrine without being a sheep, a follower of the Shepherd.

A little while back, I was listening to the Moth Radio hour on NPR. The story caught my attention because the man was clearly someone who knew the Christian scene well. He used all the buzzwords, etc. It turned out that he was the child of some Baptist missionaries and was extraordinarily gifted at apologetics and evangelism. He described how he had different strategies of engagement for different sorts of people he'd meet. Through his knowledge and gifts, he was used to lead many people to accept Jesus as their Lord and Savior. But throughout the story, you could tell there was a tension in his voice, and you just knew bad news was coming. Sure enough, he went on to tell the crowd that he eventually lost what he called "his faith" and that in spite of having all the intellectual answers, just didn't find himself comfortable being a Christian anymore.

And so, as important as doctrine is, it can't be *the thing* that separates sheep from goats. Well then, maybe it's . . .

Works?

The Bible is replete with references to the importance of our works. I mean throughout the entire Bible there are calls to obey God's law. We are called to "be holy as God is holy"— to walk uprightly, justly, and compassionately and to worship God precisely is really an important mark of Christian truth. As Jesus simply said, "If you love me, you will keep my commandments." So then, it might seem that our parable is indeed teaching that it is in fact our works that will matter most on that last day.

That seemed to be the view of Keith Green when it came to this parable. He wrote a whole song about it. (In case you don't know who he is, Green was one of the early performers in the contemporary Christian music scene in the '70s. He was immensely talented, and some of his songs are still sung in churches all across the world today). In the song, he essentially just speaks the passage over some really catchy piano grooves. When the sheep are presented, the piano part is upbeat and happy sounding. It almost makes you wanna dance (almost). But then during the goats, part the music becomes very somber and dire sounding. The judgment is handed out by Jesus, and it is just terrible. The contrast is so stark that it's hard to believe it's even the same song. What starts out as so joyous, ends so sadly. But the part that really got me the first time I listened to it were the very last words; Green shouts out, "And according to these scriptures the only difference between these two is what they did . . . and didn't . . . *do!*"

That is certainly a part of what separates the sheep from the goats in our parable. I mean, Jesus is very clear about the contrast. The sheep are those that feed, clothe, visit, and minister to "the least of these" and in doing so minister to him (a phenomenal use of language to describe Jesus's identification with the weak and seemingly worthless). We have to face facts: in the Bible (and in this parable) it's made pretty clear that this is a nonnegotiable. If you are a Christian, these things should happen.

And then on the other hand, when Jesus does describe the goats, they are those who did not do any of the ministering to the least of these. So it *cannot be denied* that our works are important indicators of our faith (as Paul and James say over and over again).

Nevertheless, the question we're seeking to answer here is what *ultimately* separates the sheep from the goats, the Christian from the non-Christian; it would seem that the rest of the Bible and indeed, even this passage give us reason to doubt that works is what ultimately separates us from God.

For starters, the Bible says over and over and over again that we are saved and will be saved, go to heaven "apart from our works" in places like Ephesians 2:9, 2 Timothy 1:9, Titus 3:5, and Romans 3:20, where it simply says, "For by works of the law no human being will be justified in his sight, since through the law comes knowledge of sin." On top of this, looking closer at our passage, please note something about these works: these lambs are surprised that their works are even noticed at all. They don't even realize they've done anything. The righteous ask, "Lord, when did we see you hungry and feed you, or thirsty and give you a drink? And when did we see you a stranger and welcome you, or naked and clothe you?" They are blown away that the King even noticed anything they did. This brings up an important point about good works: they are not something the righteous are tallying up; they are things that are almost happening unwittingly.

On the other hand, the goats, the ones who are separated from God, actually are relying on their works. Read it closely: "Then they also will answer, saying, 'Lord, when did we see you hungry or thirsty or a stranger or naked or sick or in prison, and *did not* minister to you?'" Do you hear the underlying assumption here? "When didn't we minister to you!" They are like the ones who Jesus speaks of in another passage that come to him on the last day saying, "Lord, Lord, did we not prophesy in your name, and cast out demons in your name, and do many mighty works in your name?' And then will I declare to them, 'I never knew you . . .'"

Do you see it? The goats are precisely those who come to Jesus dependent upon their works to get them in. They think they're good enough, while the sheep don't even stop to consider their works before the King. They're stunned they have anything on their record that he even notices . . .

So then what? We've determined that ultimately we won't be saved because of our doctrine. And we won't ultimately be saved even because of our good deeds. So then . . . What!

By Grace through Faith

Now, your first response may be something like this: Look, man, I'm with you. I know the Bible says that everywhere. I mean, we can't deny it, right? Ephesians 2:8 (along with numerous other passages) says clearly, "For by grace you have been saved through faith. And this is not your own doing; it is the gift of God." Nevertheless, here's my problem: I don't see it in this story of Jesus's.

You know what? I get that. At first glance when I read this story, for years I was always puzzled at how to interpret it in light of the rest of the Bible's insistence that we're saved by grace through faith alone. But I think God in his mercy turned the light bulb on for me. Here's what I mean. Look at what Jesus says to the sheep in verse 34 before he mentions any of their works: "Come, you who are blessed by my Father, inherit the kingdom prepared for you from the foundation of the world." Now stick with me here.

When was the kingdom prepared for the sheep? Jesus says, "From the foundation of the world." That word *foundation* is another way of saying even before the creation of the world. So before any works had been done, good or bad, what was God doing? Preparing a place for his sheep.

Now check out Ephesians 1:3–6

> Blessed be the God and Father of our Lord Jesus Christ, who has blessed us in Christ with every spiritual blessing in the heavenly places, even as he chose us in him before the foundation of the world, that we should be holy and blameless before him. In love he predestined us for adoption as sons through Jesus Christ, according to the purpose of his will, to the praise of his glorious grace, with which he has blessed us in the Beloved.

Put it all together. The sheep become sheep (or in this text, the sons become sons) solely by his amazing grace. But we're not done.

What are we said to be doing to get this kingdom prepared for us? We simply "inherit." What happens in an inheritance? Well to the inheritor, he or she is given something just because of his or he relationship to someone. To inherit is to receive (that is faith).

But what usually has to happen before to the one who is giving the inheritance away? They have to die, right? Now please listen again to Ephesians 1:

> In Jesus we have redemption through his blood (there's the death) the forgiveness of our trespasses, according to the riches of his grace, which he lavished upon us, in all wisdom and insight making known to us the mystery of his will, according to his purpose, which he set forth in Christ as a plan for the fullness of time, to unite all things in him, things in heaven and things on earth. In him we have obtained an inheritance, having been predestined according to the purpose of him who works all things according to the counsel of his will, so that we who were the first to hope in Christ might be to the praise of his glory. (Ephesians 1:7–14)

So you see, it is by grace through faith that we are saved, and then in turn what that produces is works for our neighbor, even the lowest of them among us.

You've probably not heard the name Allan Law before, I'm sure, but he is yet another example of a dictum I once heard; rarely are the famous good, and rarely are the good famous. Anyhow, Allan Law has garnered himself the nickname "the Sandwich Man." Why? Because every night (literally every single night of his life) since he retired sixteen years ago he has gone out from midnight to noon in the inner city of Minneapolis handing out sandwiches and other supplies to the homeless population of the city. Last year alone he personally handed out five hundred twenty thousand sandwiches, two thousand blankets, and two to three thousand pairs of socks to those in need. He has an apartment filled with seventeen freezers full of his supplies, and each night he only sleeps two to four hours. Why does he do it? Why do you think? Because he's been born again through the power of the gospel. So he says, "I truly believe that God put me on this earth to help the poor." You see, it is his faith that has overflowed into an outpouring of love for the least of those around him.

Nevertheless, we're still not done. We have important business still to take care of in regard to these goats, right? Where do they go? Listen to Jesus.

"Then he will say to those on his left, 'Depart from me, you cursed, into the eternal fire prepared for the devil and his angels.'" That sounds awful, and it is: eternal, never-ending fire. Nevertheless, even in these words of condemnation there is hope. Here's why: please notice the difference between who each of these places were prepared for. When Jesus speaks to the sheep, he says it's "for you." The kingdom, from the very beginning, was always made for his sheep. But look at who the fire was prepared for: "The devil and his angels."

Don't you see? The place where the goats are going is not a place they were ever meant to go. The place they're going wasn't prepared for them, and they don't have to go there. Why? Because God is in the business of making goats into sheep. And to the surprise of the lambs, he will work through them to feed the hungry, satiate the thirsty, welcome the stranger, clothe the naked, visit the sick, and stand with the prisoner.

Buying a Graveyard

The kingdom of heaven is like treasure hidden in a field, which a man found and covered up. Then in his joy he goes and sells all that he has and buys that field.
—Matthew 13:44

When I was ten, my brother and I found what we perceived to be a great treasure. There was a field that butted up against a small wooded area behind the townhouse where we lived. We played back there nearly every day. One day we discovered something. Just behind the tree line was the most massive pile of snack cakes we had ever seen. All different kinds. Cream-filled chocolate cupcakes. Strawberry angel food cakes. Fruit-filled pies. All still wrapped. It looked like a mountain of treats that would last the rest of our childhood.

We transported a good amount of this treasure back to the house. But someone saw us. Before we had the chance to enjoy any of it, we were informed it had been dumped there because it was expired and some of it even had worms. Treasure is in the eye of the beholder.

What Are You Willing to Give?

Throughout church history, Christians have given up everything for their faith. The history of Christianity is marked with persecution, disownment, and martyrdom. I remember reading *Foxe's Book of Martyrs* as a teenager and feeling a mix of awe and horror—story after story of men and women paying the ultimate price for their devotion to Christ.

> He is no fool who gives what he cannot keep to gain that which he cannot lose.
>
> —Jim Elliot[1]

As I heard stories about men like Jim Elliot who went into the jungles of Ecuador to evangelize the Quechua Indians and ended up speared to death, I would ask myself, could I do that? So many people giving up so much. Giving up everything. They seem to place a value on Jesus and the gospel that I'm simply not sure I do. Sure, I may say I do, but talk is cheap. I affirm that God is worthy of all glory, honor, and worship. He is the almighty Creator of all things, and nothing is more valuable or precious than being in right relationship with him. But would I give up everything? When I'm really honest, there seems to be a big difference between myself and the apostle Paul, who wrote:

> But whatever gain I had, I counted as loss for the sake of Christ. Indeed, I count everything as loss because of the surpassing worth of knowing Christ Jesus my Lord. For his sake I have suffered the loss of all things and count them as rubbish, in order that I may gain Chris. (Phil. 3:7–8)

Do you feel it—that strange mix of admiration and conviction? It's like looking at Mount Everest, knowing people before you have ascended it but realizing if your life depended on you doing the same, it's probably all over.

You Are Not the Man (or Woman)

When I've heard this parable talked about or preached on in the past, it has left me feeling guilty, questioning my devotion and even my salvation. Have I given up everything to have the treasure of Christ? Would I? Am I a fool who hasn't given what I cannot keep and therefore hasn't gained something I cannot lose? As incredible, inspiring, and admirable as the stories of Christian sacrifice are, that isn't what this parable is about. Well, that is precisely what it is about, but not in the way we think.

This is one of several parables in the thirteenth chapter of Matthew. Included in the others are the Sower, the Weeds and the Wheat, and the Mustard Seed (all of which we have already looked at). All these stories include a man and a field. When Jesus explains some of these, we find the man is the Son of God (Jesus) and the field is the world. You are not the man in any of these. I am not the man in any of these. This story is no different.

When we hear Jesus say "The kingdom of heaven is like . . ." He is about to show us that God operates in ways to make little to no sense to us. It is Jesus's go-to phrase right before he flips over all the theological tables in our mind. Our neatly organized systematic theologies and idea about God and his kingdom end up scattered on the floor. We may panic and fall to our knees to gather them up, but if we pause there, we may just get a better view of God is up to. The best view of God and his kingdom is from down in the dirt.

The Condescending God

There is a great temptation to distance God from the dirtiness of the world. We are down here in the muck and mire of sin and suffering, and he is up in the heavens somewhere in glory and righteousness, far removed from us and this fallen world. We tend to believe that we find God by ascending to him—reaching a higher level morally, spiritually, intellectually, or in any number of other ways. All religions and spiritualties do this. It's a journey of climbing spiritual ladders. But that is not how Jesus says his kingdom works.

> Being asked by the Pharisees when the kingdom of God would come, he answered them, "The kingdom of God is not coming in ways that can be observed, nor will they say, 'Look, here it is!' or 'There!' for behold, the kingdom of God is in the midst of you." (Luke 17:20–21)

Like us, the Pharisees thought of the kingdom of God as something far more glamorous than what stood before them. Jesus isn't after political power. He isn't forming relationships with people of high influence. Yet according to him, he *is* the kingdom of God in flesh and blood. It isn't what you would expect and cannot be observed with anything other than the eyes of God-gifted faith.

The kingdom of God isn't a quest man is able to embark on. He cannot find it, build it, or enter it on his own. The kingdom of God is God himself on a rescue mission in the person and work of Jesus Christ. It's the holy invasion of heaven to earth. It is God coming down low—lower than we could ever imagine him stooping. He makes his kingdom small enough to grow in the womb of a teenage girl. Humble enough to sleep where cattle and swine come to eat. Unassuming enough to dwell in a backwater town in Galilee for thirty years. Poor enough to counted with the beggars and impoverished. Shameful enough to associate with tax collectors and prostitutes. And strong enough to take on the sins of the whole world. This is what is involved in the Son of God descending to the field of this world. He is looking for something, and he knows it's somewhere in the dirt. In Jesus we see the God who comes with his sleeves rolled up. He comes to seek, save . . . and dig.

Dirty Dead Treasure

There is a large field near my house. For a few years it was full of overgrown grass and wildflowers. Nothing special was going there. One day I noticed it had cleared and the grass mowed down extremely short. I thought someone must be planning to build something. Please let it be a Chick-Fil-A! I could save so much money on gas. Maybe a cool sports bar? I need that close to my house. A few weeks passed, and then I saw it. The first gravestone in the field. I was a little disappointed. After all, a new graveyard isn't very exciting.

When Jesus finds treasure in the field of this world, it's buried. It's dirty. It's dead. It's not a treasure the world sees as valuable. It's something (someone) we buried so we wouldn't have to watch the process of decay and be overwhelmed with the smell of rot. So our memories could remain good ones. The graveyard only exists because sinners do. It cries out that things are not as they should be and "the wages of sin is death" (Romans 6:23). For us, a graveyard is a place of remembrance. For Jesus, it's a place to go to work. It's a field full of undiscovered treasure—a field all of us are born dead in.

The Bible doesn't leave room for speculation about the spiritual condition we are all born in. We are dead in sin (Eph. 2:1; Col 2:13). We are unaware that we are walking spiritual corpses. When God wraps himself in flesh and takes up residence with his creation, he becomes the first man since Adam to born spiritually alive. He is born alive to make war on the morgue, the undertaker, and the casket.

Someone sold the field near my house. But it didn't transfer owners for the last time. Jesus is in the business of buying graveyards.

The Language of Purchase

If consistency within Jesus's parables isn't enough to convince you that this story is all about him coming to the field of the world, the language of purchase should be. The man goes out and gives up everything he has to buy the field. This is incompatible with any notion that Jesus is the treasure and we are the man. The Bible's language of purchase is reserved for Christ.

> You are not your own, for you were *bought* with a price. (1 Cor. 6:20)

> And they sang a new song, saying, "Worthy are You to take the book and to break its seals; for You were slain, and *purchased* for God with Your blood men from every tribe and tongue and people and nation." (Rev. 5:9 NASB)

While the Bible and church history is full of examples of people giving up everything for the sake of Christ, any notion that what they gave up purchased or secured the kingdom of God, Christ, or salvation for them is antithetical to gospel itself. The message that God in Christ has ransomed, made atonement for, and purchased an entire world of sinners. Jesus words "It is finished" (John 19:30) are the nail in the coffin of transactional spirituality. There is nothing more to buy. Christ has purchased everything.

He bought the whole damned field and everything buried in it.

Joy and Treasure Naming

This parable is about God treading the field of this world seeking to buy dirty dead treasure with the currency of his own blood. It's a pretty staggering truth. Now add joy to that. Jesus says: *in his joy he goes and sells all that he has and buys that field.* It is like a woman who is overcome with joy after discovering she is pregnant. Joy is present along with the knowledge that without the pain of childbirth, there will be no baby to love and cherish. The author of Hebrews says: "for the joy that was set before him [Jesus] endured the cross" (Hebrews 12:2b).

The joy set before Jesus is the church. The dirty and dead people he and he alone calls "treasure." Perhaps you don't think that was a very good investment. I don't blame you. I look at the church (and at myself) and it still looks pretty dirty. It doesn't look like something capable of supplying the future joy necessary to endure horrific suffering and crucifixion. God's eyes see things in ways ours don't. He sees what he has declared to be true. You are treasure simply because he says you are. The same God who said, "Let there be light" (Genesis 1:3) and it was so, has called you treasure, and so you are. It is like a jeweler who finds a rusted metal ring and declares he has found a treasure, knowing he is going to cover it in twenty-four-carat gold and the choicest diamonds.

God has access to the joy that can endure suffering in his own power to accomplish what he has set out to do. Before we are told about this joy in Hebrews, we are told Jesus is "the author and perfecter of faith" (Hebrews 12:2a). Jesus can give up everything in joy because he is not depending on us to become more treasure-like. He is the author of our identity as treasure, and he will be the perfecter of it. He has covered us in his own righteousness and crowned us with adoption into the family of God. We are not treasure because of what we naturally are. We are treasure because of whom we are treasured by.

The Resurrection of Treasure

The treasure in the field is covered back up. We are not told that after the purchase of the field, the man went and immediately dug it up again. That is intentional. Jesus finds us dead and dirty, calls us treasure, and in joy suffering buys us. Now we wait. As time goes by, more and more treasure is buried. And we wait. More fields become graveyards. And we wait. The joy set before Jesus was the church. The hope set before us is the resurrection. This Jesus who has purchased us has promised to dig up his treasure again. On that day, what now looks dirty and dead will be righteous and immortal.

> I am the resurrection and the life. Whoever believes in me, though he die, yet shall he live. (John 11:25)

The Search for the Valuable

People are indeed looking for something of value in life. They are searching for something worth giving themselves to. The entire world is on an exhausting, endless treasure hunt. While it is true that Christ is of the utmost value, this story gives us all a much-needed message: the most valuable thing in the universe gave everything to have us. There is no earning it. There is no securing it. There is no paying him back.

One day we may be faced with giving up everything for the sake of Christ—not to gain the kingdom but because we already have it. If we are, I pray God makes us able. And we do so knowing our God is the kind of fool who gives what was his to keep to gain losers. The scandal of the story is that value is not found in us or what we do or give up. Our value is found in the God who comes down to dig around in graveyards and calls corpses treasure.

Note

1   Jim Elliot, *Shadow of the Almighty,* reissue edition (New York: HarperCollins, 2009), 108.

Daniel Emery Price is the director of Christ Hold Fast. He is an author, church and conference speaker and co-host of the podcasts *40 Minutes in the Old Testament* and *30 Minutes in the New Testament*. He has served as a church planter, pastor and worship leader and currently lives in Bentonville, Arkansas, with his wife Jessica and daughter Anna.

Erick Sorensen is a pastor and author. He earned his Master of Divinity Degree from Lutheran Brethren Seminary and has served as a Pastor in California, New Jersey and New York City. He is co-host of the podcast 30 Minutes in the New Testament. He currently lives in Succasunna, New Jersey with his wife Melissa and three sons.

Made in the USA
Las Vegas, NV
08 December 2021